WITHOUT

HER

T0188751

WITHOUT HER

a chronicle of grief and love

REBECCA SPIEGEL

MILKWEED EDITIONS

In place of pseudonyms, initials have been used throughout the text to protect the identities of the people involved beyond immediate family members.

Published 2024 by Milkweed Editions
Printed in Canada
Cover design by Mary Austin Speaker
Cover photo by Alfred Stieglitz
Author photo by Isaac Lief
24 25 26 27 28   5 4 3 2 1
First Edition

Library of Congress Cataloging-in-Publication Data

Names: Spiegel, Rebecca, author.
Title: Without her : a chronicle of grief / Rebecca Spiegel.
Description: Minneapolis : Milkweed Editions, 2024. | Summary: "A devastatingly beautiful debut memoir chronicling an emerging writer's journey through loss, grief, and a personal and familial reckoning"-- Provided by publisher.
Identifiers: LCCN 2023054683 (print) | LCCN 2023054684 (ebook) | ISBN 9781571311962 (paperback) | ISBN 9781571317704 (ebook)
Subjects: LCSH: Spiegel, Rebecca--Family. | Women authors, American--21st century--Biography. | Grief. | Sisters. | LCGFT: Autobiographies.
Classification: LCC PS3619.P5396 W58 2024 (print) | LCC PS3619.P5396 (ebook) | DDC 814/.6 [B]--dc23/eng/20240212
LC record available at https://lccn.loc.gov/2023054683
LC ebook record available at https://lccn.loc.gov/2023054684

Milkweed Editions is committed to ecological stewardship. We strive to align our book production practices with this principle, and to reduce the impact of our operations in the environment. We are a member of the Green Press Initiative, a nonprofit coalition of publishers, manufacturers, and authors working to protect the world's endangered forests and conserve natural resources. *Without Her* was printed on acid-free 100% postconsumer-waste paper by Friesens Corporation.

for my family

& for you, reader

How can I live alone, without her?

—SOPHOCLES, Ismene in *Antigone*

Grief has a life of its own and its own work to do.
It is born howling, it labors, it grows old.

—DONALD HALL, *Life Work*

I want to know about my particular grief,
which is unknowable, just like everyone else's.

—SARAH MANGUSO, *The Guardians*

WITHOUT HER

PART 1

IT WAS MARCH 26, A WEDNESDAY. I was at work and it was the sixteenth birthday of one of my students: she brought in a cake covered in white frosting, pink sugar, and black stars, and I gave her a hug and a dollar, which—as is custom in New Orleans—she added to the other bills pinned to her school uniform hoodie. She left my classroom shortly before the lunch period ended; my cell phone rang. I glanced at the screen, rolled my eyes. It was my sister Emily's college friend Z. The last time she'd reached out to me was to ask if I'd heard from Emily, but that was two months ago, a few days after my sister was admitted to an inpatient program at a psychiatric hospital.

"This can't be good," I said quietly. I stepped out into the hallway, dragged my fingers across dips in painted cinder-blocks, took the call.

"Hello?"

"Have you heard from Emily at all? I can't get hold of her." That same question—she was panicked.

"No—not for the past couple days. I sent her a G Chat message on Monday, but she never answered."

I wasn't alarmed. This wasn't new. My sister was a bit slippery, hard to keep track of. Especially lately.

"People are saying a body was found in a car on campus, and I keep trying to call Emily, but her phone keeps going to voicemail and I'm freaking out."

"Okay. Okay. Hang on. Let me try to figure out what's going on. I'll call you back," I said.

I was calm and direct, but I could feel my thinking begin to cant. I'd graduated from the same college in Colorado two years earlier, and I still had the school chaplain's number saved in my phone. I don't know why it didn't occur to me to try to call Emily.

The chaplain picked up, said, "Hello?"

"Hi, this is Becca Spiegel."

Before I could say another word, he said, "Becca, I'm so sorry . . ." I heard words like "dead" and "family" and "legally, can't initiate contact." Flooded by hot disbelief and cold certainty, I asked him if I could tell my parents to call so he could tell them what he'd just told me. Asked him to tell Emily's friend Z.

I hung up, walked straight down the hall, through two doors, outside, sat down at a picnic table, surrounded by concrete and aluminum, chain-link fence and rubber track, high school bleachers, 1.32 acres of artificial grass.

I sent two identical text messages: one to my stepfather, one to my dad. "I need you to call the college chaplain. Here is his number." The aim was neutral urgency. The shock split through my body; my mind was almost blank. Time hovered over Earth like a fog.

I called J. We'd begun dating during our senior year of college, then shared a home in New Orleans until he'd moved back to Colorado with his band two months ago, to finish writing an album and grow a vegetable garden. When I hung up, I had a missed call and new text message from Z: "The chaplains couldn't tell me anything and she's still not picking up. They said the parents might know though. I'm really sorry for calling like this."

I wrote back: "No, it's OK. Thank you for calling me. I asked the chaplain to tell you. It was her in the car. I'm so sorry."

My next thought was of the flight to South Carolina I had scheduled for the next day, to run a two-hundred-mile race from Columbia to Charleston as a member of a twelve-person relay team. I had been looking forward to the trip.

I called the captain of the team. Tried to leave a voice-mail, but erased it accidentally. Sent a text instead: "I do not think I can get on a plane tomorrow. I will explain more, but I just found out my sister died. Please tell the team I am so sorry to pull out."

I went back inside the school building, straight to the windowless office of a school social worker with whom I worked closely, Ms. A—big heart, quick wit, no-bullshit attitude. She called everyone baby in the way many Louisianans do. My discussions with her were usually about how to best support the students we shared, but sometimes we talked about her own sister's mental health history, and Emily's.

I knocked. Ms. A called for me to enter and I opened the door. She was wrapped in a cheetah-print Snuggie. (The school building was air-conditioned far too effectively.) Between us was a wide mess of desk: stacks of IEPs, framed photos of her two kids, potted plants. Tall, light-gray file cabinets where all the paperwork would end up eventually. A lamp instead of the harsh, fluorescent lights. I couldn't speak. I began to heave.

"What's wrong?" she asked.

"It's my sister . . . She's dead."

She let out a breath and hugged me. She directed me to take a seat; her office became a concrete block-and-tile sanctuary. My stepfather called. He found a way to perform calm and steady. I asked if my mother knew yet, and he said yes. I asked if I should look at flights that would get me home that night. He said to find one that worked best for me and not to think about the price.

Ms. A let me use her computer, then left to tell our principal. She returned with a gentle, well-mannered colleague and friend of mine named KC, who volunteered to take me to the airport even though it was her birthday. I accepted the offer but would not let either one of them drive me home. Insisted I was okay. Returned to my classroom, tried to shield my face from my co-teachers and the students they were helping, grabbed my bags, and left.

At the intersection of North Claiborne and Franklin, the light was red. To the left was a station that sold fresh meat, fried chicken, and discount gas. To the right, thin rectangles of fencing and wood siding in old, tired shades of yellow, white, or red. The lid of one black garbage can was propped open by too much trash. On another was written "Thou Shall Not Steal." The weather was cloudy, 55 degrees, mild wind. Bland. The ring of my phone startled me. I didn't want to answer, but I had to. It was my dad.

His voice was low and flat. He sounded tired. "What's up? I assume it's Em?"

"Did you call the chaplain?"

"No, not yet . . . What's going on? Did she try to kill herself again?"

I said, "No, Dad. She's dead."

He said, "Seriously?"

I said yes and that's all I know. Please, please call the chaplain.

I made it home. I don't know how. I can't believe I convinced anyone I could drive. And yet I was lucid. Absent-minded but thinking in tasks, in lists, in practical matters. I walked up three steps, turned a key, flipped a light switch.

It would be a few hours still before I could crumble, and even then, that's not the right word or metaphor. It's not a falling apart, either. Closer to disintegration or the chair you're sitting in breaking, giving way to the floor, but the floor's not there, and then you're not even falling, because that's too predictable, logical—you're just existing. It's not pressing pause, but nothing is playing. It's not blank, but there is nothing there. It's knowing you're boarding a plane to go home in a few hours but having no idea for how long— knowing you'll have to dress for a funeral, but what could you possibly wear?

I stuffed a bag: a black dress, boots and bras, leggings. Sneakers and headphones for the runs I assumed I'd need. A blue shirt with white embroidery that I first wore in a fitting room shared with Emily, bodies bumping in a full-length mirror as arms moved in and out of sleeves. I put on a necklace she'd gifted me and packed a pair of earrings she'd made. Toothbrush, sweatshirt, socks. All so obvious and normal, so practical and not at all.

KC WAITED WHILE I FOUND MY PHONE and wallet, turned off the lights, locked the front door. In her car, on the highway, I became aware that I had my hands clasped in my lap and could feel every single bone in them. Little wooden dowels, my skin like tissue paper, like I might break, rip, tear. Beyond that: nothing. Just glass and steel and the smooth skin of KC's hands—one on the gearshift, one on the wheel.

I looked out the window, sat very still. How had Emily distorted my words? How could I have been more clear? I was afraid that she'd left believing I didn't love her, or that I hadn't wanted her there. Had I made her feel like a burden? There was no way for me to know. So many times I looked into her eyes and thought I saw them water, but there were never any tears. When she left New Orleans, I sent her a postcard. Did she get it before she killed herself? It said, "I love you, I'm sorry, I'm so glad you were here."

As I sat at the gate, waiting to board the plane that would take me to Philadelphia, the texts started pouring in. People I hadn't spoken to in years—I didn't know how they already knew. I copy-pasted the same "thank you" to each. There was a sense of setting down a weight I hadn't known I was carrying, only to pick it up again.

Through the first two-and-a-half-hour flight, I cried quietly beneath the hood of an oversized gray sweatshirt. No one said anything or checked on me. I listened to the album *Bon Iver* on an endless loop.

During my layover at Chicago O'Hare, I walked until I found an empty waiting area by an empty gate. I located an outlet, sat on the thinly carpeted floor, and plugged in my phone. I noticed the time—it was already late, so I called my friend AJ, who lives on the West Coast. She listened as I attempted to make myself believe that this was really happening. I went to the bathroom and looked in the mirror: lids swollen, dark circles beneath, like I'd been punched generously in both my eyes. I got on another plane and continued to cry.

It was 1 a.m. by the time I landed in Philadelphia. I'd asked my father to pick me up from the airport and drive me to my mother's house in Delaware. I stood waiting at the arrivals curb beneath lights far too bright. It was just below freezing. I wrapped my gray hoodie tightly around my body.

I soon spotted a navy-blue Prius. My stepmother was driving; my father opened the passenger door, extended his arms to me, and said, "I'm so sorry," as if his own pain were irrelevant. For most of the next twenty-five minutes, we rode in silence. Nothing registered, not even the dark—it could have been any time of day, on any planet, in any year.

The Prius pulled into the driveway of my mother and stepfather's house. A motion sensor registered our presence, and a small floodlight screamed from the upper left corner of the garage. My stepmother said, "Good night, sweetie." My dad told me to try to get some sleep.

"I'll try. Get home safely. I'll talk to you tomorrow. I love you."

I closed the car door and turned toward the house. The windows were dark, but the front door was unlocked. It squealed as I closed it behind me, and my heart beat as if I'd broken curfew. I walked down a hallway—past the stairs that led to the basement, past the kitchen on my left, the office on my right, past a bathroom. From the doorway of my mother and stepfather's room, I could see two lumps beneath a down comforter. I didn't know whether to climb into their bed or go upstairs to my own room. It seemed safest to stay silent.

My mom muttered my name. I took two steps into the room and was by her side of the bed. I leaned down to hug her and felt her hair damp with tears, her forehead oily, her cheek warm and puffy against mine.

When I opened my eyes the next morning, I felt a dull, constrictive sting. I lay on my side, adjusting to the thin line of sunlight between the windowsill and the blinds. Too quickly, I remembered where I was and why. I sat up and looked at myself in the mirror above my old dresser, adorned with books I had yet to read, a frosted bottle of the pink perfume I wore in high school, and a small collection of junk mail sent to me at my parents' address. I needed ice and coffee.

I descended the burgundy carpeting of the staircase, holding tight to the banister's wood. In the kitchen were my mother, stepfather, and Aunt K, my mother's friend of thirty years. As soon as I'd gotten the news, I called K. I knew my mom would need her. She'd taken a red-eye from Los Angeles and had just arrived.

I hugged each one of them tight, then took a bag of green peas out of the freezer and held it over one eye. I sat on a stool at the high-top table, joining my mother and Aunt K. My stepfather poured coffee from a stainless steel French press, offered me the mug. I lowered my face over the steam, my uncovered eye on my mom. We were both in our pajamas, our phones face up on the table. New messages appeared on both screens in steady streams. I removed the bag of peas, blinked intensely several times, and covered my other eye. I asked, "Did you guys get any sleep?" but all I got were shrugs. No one said much. What was there to say? Aunt K answered the landline when it rang. We were each our own impenetrable system, states of matter cycling—solid, liquid, gas.

That afternoon, my mother and father had an appointment at a funeral home. My mother didn't feel fit to drive; despite my dread, I volunteered. My parents had spent most of my life hating each other, and they'd just lost a child. As I pulled my mother's SUV into a small parking lot behind the memorial chapel, a three-story home made of beige stone, I braced for a fight over a casket or urn, or the cost of the funeral. Across the street were a liquor store and paint center. Had the three of us ever been in the same place and been so impassive? My mother seemed reduced next to me, like boiled down sugar water. A petite body, blue eyes, brown hair. I walked over to my father, wrapped desperate arms around his middle. To do so in front of my mother felt strange and logical. My forehead brushed the copper-white wires of his long goatee; he smelled, as ever, of Listerine. When I stepped back, his bright brown eyes were dull and tender behind their frames—no trace of their habitual glare.

The funeral director wore a suit and tie. We followed him through a narrow hallway with somber lighting. I watched and listened as he showed us models of caskets—equal parts salesman and counselor. My mother said mostly nothing; my father said "cremation." The director extended an arm, told us to have a seat. My father and I took the two chairs in front of the director's desk, while my mother faded into a plaid love seat in the background. The director handed us a catalog of urns, the whole range, very fancy to very plain. I stopped paying attention. On the corner of the desk were a flimsy box of tissues and a ceramic pot containing a pink orchid that I couldn't make sense of. It was papery. It was dead.

We departed the funeral home together. I hugged my father again and told him I'd see him soon. My mother and I got into her car. Stop signs, traffic lights, the click of the turn signal. It all felt far away.

That night I woke at an odd hour and turned from my side to stomach to back, wishing to not be conscious. The handful of plastic stars on the ceiling of my childhood bedroom glowed in the dark. J, who had arrived a few hours earlier, lay next to me, sound asleep. I grabbed my iPad, walked out of the bedroom and down the stairs without turning on a light. On the sunroom sofa, I wrapped myself in a blanket, turned on the device: a stream of public tributes to my sister filtered through blue light. To see how others were memorializing her on social media inspired both comfort and contempt—I wanted my pain to be shared, but particular to me, unique. I wanted them to remember that I was the one for whom this loss was truly devastating.

At 4:23 a.m., I posted:

> For anyone who, like me, is searching for something to do to honor Emily's life, three potential options come to mind:
>
> First, with compassion and kindness, you can do your best to take care of yourself and the people around you.
>
> Second, you can talk about it—whatever "it" is for you. This is an important part of number one.
>
> And third, you can donate to Grow: Mental Health Support and Advocacy for College Students.

What was it about this performance that I found comforting? It was almost an act of complicity, as if the illogic of the loss, the experience of emptiness, made a public gesture both indecent and necessary. I started to feel tired. I went back upstairs.

WHEN I RETURNED TO THE SUNROOM in the morning, my mother, stepfather, father, stepmother, and the rabbi responsible for my and Emily's Jewish education were all sitting on the same sectional sofa, beige and microsuede. I sat on the floor next to a wicker basket filled with the past month's newspapers and studied the bronze edge of the coffee table, a relic from my mother and father's life predivorce.

"Sorry," I said. "I overslept." The rabbi explained how the funeral service would go. I was the only one among us who said they'd like to give a eulogy. My parents took turns answering the rabbi's questions, describing Emily. Outside, it was either foggy or raining lightly. It all felt fake: the words, the setting, their faces. Four pairs of glasses, their hands plastic, their noses beige.

My stepfather's jaw tensed before he spoke. "Everything was a project." His light brown eyes brightened, voice steady with conviction. "She was always thinking. Always."

I rolled my eyes.

My father went wide-eyed as he spoke of spirits and energy. My stepmother kept to herself by his side. Her clear blue eyes were rimmed with red, her blond hair flat and fine. My father gesticulated reverence and said something about Emily ascending to be with the angels.

I wished for a blanket to wrap myself in tightly so that I could hide my disdain.

"Are you serious?"

The moment grew taut and the rabbi slid right through it, offering my father validation. I refused to contribute further to the conversation.

When the rabbi stood up to leave, he asked me to come with him. I followed out the front door and down three steps, into clouds and wind. Standing on the path of slate, he turned toward me, his whole tall frame, put one of his hands on my shoulder. This man had known me for years, had told me many times he held me in high regard. His voice was deep and firm, often sarcastic but not unkind. I waited for gentle words. He looked down and fixed round, brown eyes on mine. "It's not okay to speak to your father the way you did back there. He didn't do anything wrong—everyone here is hurting."

All I could hear was reproval. I felt indignant, full of shame.

When we were young, I made Emily play school with me in her bedroom. From a chest of dress-up clothes, I'd pull out high heels far too large and create spelling quizzes for my sister and stuffed animal pupils, then grade them with stickers and smiley faces. At night, I lay in my bed while a parent read to me. I remember best the books' covers: the regal, striped wallpaper on *A Little Princess* and *The Secret Garden*'s shiny bright green. After they turned out the lights, our mother sang "You Are My Sunshine," her voice sweet and a bit off-key; our father sang "House at Pooh Corner"—during the chorus we'd tell the clouds, "Get out of the sky!" They'd kiss me good night and leave my bedroom door open a crack, and I'd lie on my back, watching the twilight sky through my window, listening to the joyous yelps of the bigger kids on the block, still playing outside. I prayed in a whisper, or perhaps only in my head, for my family to be kept safe and healthy. In the mornings, I'd enter my parents' room. I liked the sunlight that covered their bed and the way the quilt looked like a tent whose poles were my father's long, bent legs.

When I broke a rule or misbehaved, I was sent to the steps for a time-out. Once, when I was four or five, I sat there, on carpeted basement stairs, rolling a stink bug between my fingers. I hadn't known what it was until it was too late: a sharp insect smell, like rotting furniture and acid, burrowed into my skin. From where I sat I could see and hear the TV. The local news was on, a segment about dads in jail, and their kids looked so sad to me. I knew my dad got mad easily, and my mom had made threats to call the police, so I began to carry a fear of my father behind bars and me and my little sister visiting him there.

My earliest memory of a fight between my parents begins before a backdrop of wallpaper, white squares, thin blue lines. I sat at the kitchen table, and Emily was strapped into her blue high chair in the corner of the room. It was dinner-time. My father stood at the counter, cutting a loaf of bread. My mother said, "You're not doing it right." From there, they began to fight over which way to slice it. We sat small and invisible, Emily and I—watched two pairs of hands and the blade of one knife until my mother escaped my father's grip. He followed when she left the room, and so did I.

They wrestled on the ugly gray basement carpeting until my mother reached a corded phone. I ran over and held down the button that kept the phone circuit closed, making a call impossible. She told me to let it go. I didn't. I didn't want my mom to call the police, my dad to go to jail.

By the time the lights, blue and red, streamed through the glass windows by the front door, I was back upstairs with Emily, who was still strapped into her high chair. I tiptoed down again to watch what was happening, our cat beside me, his bones beneath my fingers, his fur white and black. I wanted him to read my mind, to be the one to protect and take care of me.

When they told us they were splitting up, I was almost six and Emily had only just turned three. We were in the living room, sitting on a blue-and-peach-colored rug. How did they explain it? Did they tell us they loved us, that it wasn't our fault? Did they promise not to put us in between? We wanted to know which one of them was going to keep the dog. The dog moved into an apartment with our dad. Our mom kept the cat. Of us they had joint custody.

I prefer to remember the trips to Maine during which our father and stepmother took Emily and me to spend a week with his side of the family—our aunt and uncle and their three kids, and our grandparents. It was a tradition for four or five years. There were several reasons why we stopped going: one was that my father and his older brother kept getting into arguments, another was that we eventually had other obligations—things like marching band camp and field hockey preseason two-a-days. But while it lasted, it was so much fun. The five kids, all close in age, asked the ocean to send us big waves by twirling in circles, water up to our waists, and yelling, "Come on—is that the best you've got?" We wore striped bathing suits all week, and when we weren't in the water or building sandcastles or playing other games, we chased one another around the rented house where we stayed—bare feet on green grass, pink water balloons, and neon squirt guns—until one of us, almost always the youngest, ran away in tears.

The best part was the one morning each year when my father woke us up before the sun. We dressed each other in the sweaters and jeans we'd laid out the night before, then let ourselves be carried across the street onto the beach. We lay

down on the cold sand and waited for the light, quiet and too
sleepy to do much besides find comfort in each other's bodies.
The start of the day all ours, the sand unblemished and the
sky a pink miracle of less interest than the patches of beach
we liked to explore—the bits that smelled like old fish where
our tiny, tanned legs sank down into the cool, damp world
beneath our feet.

Two nights before the funeral, a neighbor or friend or some designated nice lady from the synagogue brought a challah over to my mother's house for Shabbat dinner. There was an assortment of people: my mother's sister, a collection of close friends—Emily's, our mother's, mine. The temperature had jumped up to sixty degrees, so we decided to eat outside. The backyard began with a stone patio, beyond which was a wide green lawn that I used to mow, with a redbud tree that bloomed rosy pink outside my bedroom window. Beyond the lawn were a red toolshed, a tire swing, the tree fort Emily and I helped our stepfather build, a hammock, creek, and woods.

My mother asked everyone to participate in our family's Shabbat tradition: as the challah is passed around the table, each person tears off a piece and shares something for which they are thankful. First for our own amusement, then later as an act of teenage rebellion when forced to sit through family dinners on Friday nights, Emily and I would say "stuff and things" as we took fistfuls of soft, eggy dough. That night, though, everyone was sincere. We all said we were thankful to be here, together, to be able to be here together. I felt so unbearably present and so deeply absent at the same time. We were not somber—there was laughter. To reconcile the joy with the occasion was impossible, but it didn't matter— there was no pretense, no one cared. The sun disappeared.

We drank beers and built a fire, told funny stories, smoked weed using a green apple as a pipe. It was what Emily would have wanted. Or was it? Did it matter? She wasn't there.

Inside, later, there was music: J's voice harmonizing with someone else's, a Steve Winwood song. The piano hadn't been tuned in who knows how long, maybe ever. I disappeared into Emily's room. I opened the drawers of her desk, a feminine blond wood thing with floral details, which matched the furniture in the rest of the room.

The top drawer was full of pens and markers. In the middle drawer were stacks of CDs by bands that were my favorite in high school, like Third Eye Blind and Death Cab for Cutie, which I'd burned for her. In the bottom drawer were piles of photos and a few old diaries. I stood there for a while, flipping through the photos. Then I gathered what I'd found into my arms and brought it all downstairs to the dining room table.

Two of Emily's friends, two of mine, and J joined me. We sat in wooden chairs and sifted through rectangles strewn across the table, a tag sale of paper memories. We laughed at the silly faces Emily made for the camera. I opened a notebook with a peace sign and flowers and "Peace&Love" on its sherbet tie-dye cover and began to read eleven-year-old Emily's diary, her handwriting clean and loopy.

Even then, she was depressed and too busy. She wrote about the boys she liked, how much she hated having divorced parents and traveling back and forth between houses. She wrote that our mom and stepfather were pissing her off and our father was "just an asshole (to put it plainly)." She criticized herself harshly and made resolutions like "lose weight" (to go from "probably like 108" to her goal weight of 95 pounds), "control snacking (NO SNACKING!!!!!)," "learn to be nicer," and "stand up / speak my mind to Dad."

My own eleven-year-old thoughts had been similar. To describe how I felt about our parents, I'd written the word "hate" fifty-six times. I called myself ugly and fat, fretted over how I would perform in swim meets, lamented unrequited elementary school love.

Except to note how annoying she was, I hardly ever wrote about Emily. Once I wrote that she was better than me at softball; once I wrote that my stepfather saved her when she almost drowned beneath a wave; once I wrote that I missed her; once I wrote that she was losing her mind. Growing up, people used to tell us that one day we'd be friends, but we did not get along. I hated when Emily followed me or tried to get my attention. I hated when anyone did anything mean to her when "anyone" wasn't me. I wanted to protect her. I wanted her to stop bothering me. I remembered myself as a typical, bossy older sister: not nice, but not wicked. I kept reading to see what she'd written about me.

Emily recorded that I'd given her three training bras I didn't wear anymore (a good thing), that I was ******* and a ☺!?#@ and evil (a bad thing), and that I was constantly calling her a loser "and telling me I'm stupid or the things I do are stupid. I know it's not true, but it really hurts my feelings, and she does it on a daily basis. Why does she not like me so much?"

I put the diary down on the dining table and pressed my head hard into my hands, trying to rub the tears into my skin. I couldn't take anything back or apologize. I detached completely from my body, where I was and what I was doing. I peeled my hands from my face, picked the book back up, and continued to turn pages. I sifted through the sentences clinically. I only stopped when I got to a passage about D, her childhood best friend, who was sitting across from me.

annoys me
occasianally, but he's
thinking of commiting suicide.
I don't want him too. My
aunt, Aunt Stephanie
commited suicide, but I wish
she didn't. I think she would
have been a really good aunt.
Mom said she had like a

disease or samething that
made her depressed. I
feel bad for Mom. I grieve
over my dead pets, but
Mom has to get over a dead
sister. But not just a
peaceful death, a suicide.

I passed the diary to D and watched his face as he read. When he finished he looked up, met my gaze, and let out a long breath, shaking his head very gently.

ON SATURDAY I SLEPT IN, then went for a run through nearby parks and neighborhoods. It helped to get out of the house, to put it all on pause. When I returned, my mother told me that my sister's body had arrived in Delaware, and she asked me to find an outfit in which the undertaker could dress Emily for one final goodbye before the cremation.

I looked through Emily's dresser drawers and closet, but there was not much to choose from: dresses worn to high school dances (one of which was mine), droopy threadbare sweaters, a pair of turquoise suede high heels, breezy tank tops marked by splotches of paint. Neither of us had left much behind when we left for college. Neither of us had planned to return home for more than a suitcase-long visit. I walked back to my room, opened my bag. Picked a pair of black leggings, stretchy, sure to fit. The indigo shirt I'd tried on with her in the folds of a shared dressing room; she'd bought it, too, in ivory, so I knew she would approve in real life.

Downstairs, I found Uncle B, another of my mother's closest friends. He'd driven in from Manhattan. He stood at the kitchen counter, tall and lean, dark-haired and clean-shaven, framed by a wide bay window and a collection of blue glass jars and figurines. The yellow stars of daffodils trumpeted from vases on the windowsill. Uncle B took a knife to the flesh of an eggplant, the corners of his lips and eyes pinched in concentration. He laid each round slice on a metal sheet, sprinkled them with kosher salt, and set them aside. Their bitter juices needed an hour to weep, so we went to the liquor store to buy slivovitz. I'd never heard of it—the name sounded like a slimy species of fish. My uncle explained that it's a plum spirit that Jews customarily drink as a part of the funeral rites.

I walked into the store and felt overwhelmed instantly. Thousands of bottles, fluorescent lights; I was unequipped to think, unable to make a choice. I stepped outside to wait and traced the dips and spikes of the popcorn walls. I noted the three empty parking spots, tilted my eyes up toward the blue roof and gray sky. Maybe I'd never been to a real Jewish funeral, I realized. When my maternal grandfather died after a lengthy decline, my grandmother invited people over to their house by the beach and called it a celebration of life. When a high school classmate was shot and killed, I walked from wooden church pew to open casket. When a friend's mother died of cancer, I stood, sat, and knelt beneath stained glass windows and intersecting barrel vaults. Never before had the hurt been so unmistakably mine.

We returned with cardboard boxes of bottles—not just slivovitz but Scotch, beer, wine—which were set down in the kitchen. Uncle B preheated the oven to 400 degrees. He flipped each slice of eggplant in a bowl of egg yolks and breadcrumbs, took jars of red sauce and tipped them gently, released fistfuls of mozzarella cheese. The sun was setting, and visitors began to arrive: the neighbors I'd met as an eleven-year-old Girl Scout selling cookies, whose house smelled warm and rich like brisket; names and faces I didn't recognize; friends of the family; former teammates from high school field hockey. It was nice and strange to see all these people who, for so long, had existed only as memories. It was nice and strange and overwhelming and there was nowhere else I could imagine being and nowhere else I'd rather be less, and I had to escape because I was out of words and out of energy, weary of hugs and the words "I'm so sorry." I wandered back upstairs to my room, closed the door to light and sound—without body, without sleep, without understanding. I didn't understand, didn't know, didn't want to know, what was happening.

THE FUNERAL SERVICE WAS HELD at a quarter to one on Sunday. It was raining. I wore a black dress to which a black ribbon was pinned to mark my mourning. It was the same dress I'd worn on my very first day teaching. The funeral scene was lifted from a movie, complete with never-ending receiving line. I stood next to my father and the rest of my family, shook hands by the hundreds, and tried to suck dry from each pair of eyes all emotion, unsure whether my role was to comfort or be comforted.

The service started. The rabbi stood at a lectern on a bimah carpeted in a light, mossy green. On the wall behind him were twelve stained glass crowns: identical jewels of sharp blue with curls of orange and buds of green, round purples, restless yellows. I listened to him describe Emily. His words were convenient, imprecise. When he talked about our relationship as sisters, he mixed up the key details. I was the one who, at the age of seven, had completed the prompt "If the dinosaurs came back . . ." with "I think it would bite me sistre head oof"—not Emily.

When it was my turn to speak, I walked up to the lectern, iPad in hand, and scanned several dozen rows of neatly seated bodies. Of all the faces, only those of the college's president and dean were not indistinct. I felt grateful they were there. And resentful, sure, and scared.

"The last time Emily was standing up here was during her confirmation, when she was sixteen. Being Emily, of course, she treated her captive audience to a speech about peanut butter and jelly sandwiches. Today, though, I am going to read two things that I think she would have wanted you to hear. The first is a blog post she wrote for GROW—the student organization she helped lead that advocates for mental health in our college community—when she was twenty. It's titled 'On Giving Too Much.'"

I keep hearing that I need to take care of myself. Sure. Got it. But what about everyone else?

In the past week, I have spent time taking care of a far too drunk friend and listening to her process it the next day, quietly sitting with a friend in crisis, meeting with an acquaintance to discuss anxiety and eating woes, talking to two practical strangers about anxiety and depression until the wee hours of the night, and attending a NAMI (National Alliance on Mental Illness) event at which I felt my heart rubbing raw with attendees' stories. The list goes on.

I enjoy listening, doing my best to help, and utilizing my experiences as a sort of cathartic pseudo-therapy. But what are the risks of opening yourself up as a resource who is, to an extent, well-versed in a number of mental health issues?

I don't sleep as much as I need to, for starters. I always try to say that I will be clear when I am not available or can't help if that's the case, but it happens less often than maybe it should. I *can* listen to my friend process a family crisis for two hours. Will I sleep less? Work longer hours in the printshop? Yes. But am I capable and willing to assist in whatever way I can? Absolutely. Should I? I'm not sure.

It's supposed to be that old adage that I need to listen to: you can't help others until you help yourself . . .

and yet I can't seem to figure out where to draw that line. I opened myself up when I assisted with a talk about wellness to the incoming class during New Student Orientation. I spoke fervently about the need to decrease stigma—to be more open, vulnerable, and honest. So I told approximately five hundred people a small part of my story. And since then, I feel loaded down with secrets, confessions, fears, and mental health struggles. I am not a therapist, and I am not necessarily qualified to help those who share with me.

I am happy to help. It helps me, in a lot of ways, to know that I am capable of connecting with others, the inability to do so being one of my greatest fears. But I'm tired, and I suppose I have to learn to listen without my whole heart. Part of my heart belongs to me, right? I'm even afraid to post this, afraid that some of these people that have reached out so bravely will read this and shy away. That's not the point; rather, writing this is my way of processing my own feelings of a heavy load. Maybe this is also my way of warning those who give of themselves to a point of detriment. Talking about mental health is hard; but for me, watching out for my own may be even harder.

"And this is from her diary when she was eleven."

I occasionally don't like my life, but I know that if I stick with it, I could do something great, like save an endangered species. So I know I should keep going along. I wonder when my first kiss will be. Did Becca get hers yet?? That's none of my business. From now on I vow never to read anyone's diary. I would be furious if someone read mine.

"Emily, I'm sorry if I made you furious, and I honestly don't know if I'd gotten my first kiss yet. But what I do know is that even though you couldn't stick with it anymore, or keep going along, if you were here today you'd see that you truly have done something great. I'm proud of you and I love you, no matter what."

I left the bimah and returned to my seat, unsure of what I'd just said, my body a miniature earthquake. In front of me, beside the lectern, was a basket overflowing with fresh flowers. I wondered why anyone had bothered. Decoration didn't matter and decorum didn't make anything better, didn't make me feel better, didn't change anything.

The reception that followed the funeral service was held in the auditorium of the local Jewish community center where Emily and I had both attended preschool. The room hadn't changed much: the floor was newly covered with a thin gray-blue carpet, and an overcoat of white had been applied to the walls' dark, vertical paneling. Front and center was a royal-blue velvet curtain that hung over a stage where I'd once had the lead role in a third-grade play. There were collapsible tables arranged in four long rows, banquet-style. They were covered in tablecloths and littered with bright, multicolored plates and napkins, sunflowers for center-pieces, platters of hoagies, and stacks of pizza boxes. Almost a party, save for the lighting, dim and confused, and the hush of the room. Emily's friend A had created a playlist of music that might have given the occasion a lively gloss, but the sound system wasn't working, so instead there was chatter and chewing, dull paper plates filled with food. I couldn't eat—less because I had no appetite than because I felt obligated to circulate, to thank each person for attending and receive each condolence thrust upon me, to answer questions politely as if my life existed outside of this room, as if it were something I would soon casually resume.

The next stop was my father's house. The day before he'd texted me, "I have one request of you," and it was that I attend this gathering he'd decided to host, separately, for his side of the family. It was redundant, and I was exhausted, but I'd messed up when I cut him off during the conversation with the rabbi, and I felt guilty that I'd only been spending time at my mother's house, where I felt more at home, and, anyway, I was closer with my father's side of the family.

J accompanied me, as did our friend JC, and a whole crew of Emily's friends from college who'd flown in, including Z. When we walked in through the front door, to our left was the living room, eight empty folding chairs arranged in a circle in the center of an olive-green rug. To our right was the dining room, a table covered with round platters of deli meat. I wasn't hungry, and I didn't know what to do. I stood around in the terra-cotta-colored kitchen. The round high-top table where we usually sat to eat was occupied by liters of Pepsi, Sprite, 7UP, and seltzer. Also apple juice, ice melting in a crystal bowl, an untouched stack of plastic cups. There was a collection of black magnets on the refrigerator, and beneath one I noticed a piece of paper upon which my stepmother had written a grocery list. What recipe calls for crowns of broccoli, sticks of carrots, stalks of celery? Could we resurrect the body? Skin grafted from apples, each birthmark a blueberry? How simple it would be to unlatch the lid of an egg carton, poke each oval, check for any guts that might have leaked.

"Hi."

I turned around and saw J and his mother and sister. His whole family had come over to my father's house—an act consistent with their generosity.

We chatted about the service: yes, so many people, yes, so beautiful. I asked J's mother to take a picture of her son and me. In the photos, J is stiff by my side and I appear wildly happy and wholly unaware of the one garnet bra strap that has slipped off my shoulder and escaped my starched sleeve.

J's father walked over and joined us. He'd just emerged from the underworld of the unfinished basement, the place my father visits regularly when not working or trimming hedges or watching Sixers or Giants or Mets or Philadelphia Union games on TV. J's father grabbed a cookie, then suddenly fell, hit his forehead on the kitchen counter on his way down, and began to bleed onto the tile floor.

My first thought was heart attack. My second was disbelief in the form of a plea: *Not more death already, not today, please, no one in this house can handle another tragedy.* My third thought was *Thank god J's mother and sister are doctors.* My fourth was to call 911. My fifth was *What if the police come with the ambulance? They'll go down to the basement and see a few bare light bulbs, gray paint peeling from concrete, dust-covered shelves filled with board game boxes, a green Ping-Pong table, two stools and a folding chair, a large silver volcano-shaped vaporizer, and all my father's marijuana. Jail.*

By the time EMS arrived, J's father, also a doctor, had regained consciousness. He declined treatment, later explaining to us that he must have gotten lightheaded after accidentally getting way too high. Once it was clear he really was okay, just embarrassed, I stayed a little longer, then hugged each of my relatives goodbye.

J drove us back to my mother's house in the dark. Shortly after he made the left onto her street, but still a good distance from the driveway, we saw the string of parked cars. The house itself was tightly packed. People were sitting anywhere—couches, rugs, stools, stairs. My ninth-grade Spanish teacher, tenth-grade English teacher, and eleventh-grade chemistry teacher arrived in a pack and stood in my kitchen, just regular people who cared. An elementary school friend's mother (who was now married to the sixth-grade

teacher Emily and I had both idolized) set a cake carrier full
of miniature zucchini muffins on the kitchen table beside me.
I stood and ate them without thought, one by one, sticky and
moist, until my friend H linked her arm with mine and pulled
me into the office across the narrow hall.

. The room was one giant built-in desk and two windows
opposite a wall of built-in cabinets and shelves containing
childhood picture books; the textbooks my stepfather had
accumulated over decades of teaching chemistry to undergraduates; novels by Edward Abbey, Italo Calvino, Barbara
Kingsolver, Gabriel García Márquez, Toni Morrison,
Salman Rushdie, the Russian greats; and the Harry Potter
series—which, when we were kids, our mother and stepfather
took turns reading to us on Saturday mornings or Sunday
afternoons, snuggled in their bed. We'd beg them for just
one more chapter, then sneak the book into our own rooms
to read ahead.

H slid shut the office's pocket door. J and Aunt K and
Uncle B and D and A were already there, all grown up, passing around a condolence gift someone had brought.

"I can't talk to any more people," said my aunt.

"It's amazing how many are here," said my uncle.

"I want some," I said, reaching for the bottle of Scotch. I
let the swallow sting, tried not to breathe. This was comforting. There was ease. We teased my uncle, laughing about
the mess he'd made in the kitchen the day before. This was
where I wanted to be. This was where I wanted to stay.
Right here, in this moment, on this blue braided rug, sitting
with these people I love, drinking something meant to be
savored, not pulled. I wanted never to have to talk to or see
anyone else. The funeral was over and the house was too
crowded, but soon they'd all go and this place would be so
quiet, so unbearably cold.

ON THE MORNING THAT FOLLOWED THE FUNERAL, I was awakened by touch, a hand on my back. It was my mother's mother, whom I call Bubbie—she'd just arrived. She had missed the service because when Emily died she was on a boat on the Mekong River—seventy-six and very alive—fisheries and rice paddies and large barges passing by. She couldn't get home in time.

"Oh, my love, I'm so sorry," Bubbie said softly. She hugged me; I began to cry. This woman's very essence is vitality: a high school art teacher turned volunteer museum docent who wears art fair jewelry and an Apple Watch, is persistently eager to discuss books we've read, and is fond of potato chips and chocolate ice cream. Here she was, holding me, yet for her, Emily's suicide compounded pain generationally—a fresh cut in a thirty-one-year-old wound. Some part of me knew the ghost of my mother's oldest sister was there in the room.

Bubbie got up to grab me a tissue for the snot I was blowing into my pillowcase. I thanked her, then said I was going to get dressed and join everyone downstairs. She left. I continued to lie in my bed for some time, then out of nowhere felt bite marks on my skin, a need to move. Changed into spandex shorts and a sports bra. Went down as many stairs as possible, past the fruit baskets and flowers left floating in the wake of the funeral.

When we'd moved into this house thirteen years before, not long after our half sibling, Ches, was born, our mother and stepfather let Emily and me choose the paint for the basement. She was seven, I was ten. Two walls were bright yellow, two walls were bright blue. We'd spent a lot of time down there separately—either hanging out with our friends or "watching movies" (making out). When Emily and I were in the basement together, we ate bowls of popcorn or frozen berries and rewatched our go-to movies (*Eternal Sunshine of the Spotless Mind, Good Burger, Ever After, Remember the Titans*) or spoke to each other in a gibberish language we'd adopted from our favorite computer game, *The Sims*, until we were laughing so hard our stomachs ached and we fell to the floor, barely able to breathe.

As she got older, Emily became more interested in spending time with the person she was dating than with me—I'd come down the basement stairs to switch my laundry from the washer to the dryer and see them cuddling by the light of the TV screen, then complain to my mother that my sister only wanted to hang out with her high school boyfriend (or, during senior year, her girlfriend), never with me.

I picked up a remote, sat on the stationary bike, and gave myself a test: I selected the next episode of *House of Cards* and hit play. I began to pedal. My limbs loosened, my jaw dissolved into static, my ribcage calcified. Of course the plot carried on. Of course I could watch either way.

The episode ended. I got off the bike. Stood dripping sweat. I heard the basement door open. My mother appeared. First her wool socks, then her blue jeans—she paused halfway down the stairs, crouched down so she could see me.

"What's going on?" she said.

I didn't speak.

Our eyes seemed to meet, but I stared past her face and my mind jumped to J, to the time he and my sister had spent together over the course of the two years we'd been dating. During Emily's last inpatient hospital stay, two months before she died, J was in Colorado and I was in New Orleans, far away. When she was released, he drove two hours to see her, took her to a drive-in hamburger joint and convinced her to get a banana milkshake. Even managed to make her smile once. He told me she'd seemed so sad, so removed, that one smile felt like a victory.

But he'd also known her happy and stable—mini music festivals at the college we all attended, Ches's b'nai mitzvah, the party J's parents threw for his sister when she graduated from medical school, a dinner at the White Dog Cafe, the drive J and Emily had made together the previous summer from Delaware to Maine. He knew the ways we mirrored each other, including our laugh, how we sat in the last row of our mother's minivan and giggled ourselves into a separate, sillier existence. Emily adored J for his gentle nature, his sincerity, his punny sense of humor, how much he adored me. Her favorite joke to make was "Your kids are going to look like troll dolls" in reference to his short stature and long, thick, curly hair. The image that came to mind every time was a child with a bejeweled belly button, big eyes, and a tall tuft of neon-orange hair.

"Becca?"

I startled—felt myself shiver, drenched in cooling sweat. My mother was standing in front of me. The sight of her made me wonder: What had she seen in my father? Why had she married him? A tall, auburn-haired boy from New York with golden-brown eyes, a lean and muscular frame. They met in college. Freshmen. His life must have seemed so quiet compared to hers: she was the youngest of four siblings, one of whom died while she was in high school, her oldest sister in and out of hospitals, ill for seven years—

doctors, counselors, pills—then, in the end, a gun in the mouth. I know the chaos a sister like this brings. The way her illness monopolizes your family's attention, makes you feel invisible, or like you should be. Like you can't add any more to anyone's plate—their plates, your plate, you're so full already and so empty too. I know the void there. My father loves to give: gifts, attention, care.

I spoke as if possessed. "This means I can never date anyone except J."

"What do you mean?"

"No one else will ever really know me. They won't know Emily."

My mom tried to hug me, but I didn't want to be touched. I turned away from her and walked up the basement stairs.

THE END OF MARCH TURNED TO APRIL: my little cousin's seventh birthday. The day was warm and sunny, and my last in Delaware. My mother's house was littered with sunflowers in mason jars and vases. J made a batch of Bloody Marys with Tabasco and lemon. My mother and Bubbie and my great-aunt and great-uncle drank them from plastic cups on the back patio. My mother's sister brought out a cupcake and lit a candle, and we all sang to her son. To celebrate felt natural and wrong, like biting off a piece of my own body.

On the plane back to New Orleans, I sat in a middle seat, sandwiched between two middle-aged men. When the flight attendant asked if we'd like a beverage, both of the men ordered craft beers, then insisted I let them also order one for me. They asked me what I did and I told them I was a high school special education teacher, then they asked where I was from and I said Delaware, then they asked if I had siblings and I described my half sibling, who had just attended their eighth-grade formal dance, and my sister, a junior at the same college in Colorado that I had graduated from two years earlier. Yes, we're very close; no, she didn't go there because of me; sure, okay, maybe she really did want to follow me out West. Emily's absence almost felt real then because I was lying. I was describing my dead sister to them and they didn't know. Our drinks came and the man in the window seat said, "Cheers!" I held the tab of the aluminum can between my thumb and forefinger, pushed it forward and back, felt it weaken until it was barely there. The man in the window seat asked for my number when the plane landed, and I typed it into his phone. Easier than saying I have a boyfriend or just plain no.

Outside, it was dark and late. My friend JK picked me up and drove me home. I wouldn't be there for more than a day: I'd long ago bought a ticket to Colorado to visit J and our dog—and Emily. There wasn't much point in going anymore, but I felt neither ready to be alone nor functional enough to return to work. In the morning, I unpacked and repacked my bag. There was still time to fill. I took my car to a car wash, a thing I rarely do. The soap and spray were methodical. I lay down and tried to nap. I boarded another plane.

When J picked me up at the airport in Denver, I tossed my bag into the trunk of his Volkswagen Jetta hatchback and then flopped myself into the passenger seat. Reached across the gear shift to give him a hug—he put up a hand to stop me.

"I haven't been feeling great," he said. I could hear his stuffed and runny nose. He said his head and throat both ached, then smiled shyly as he opened the car's center console. "This might help, though," he said, producing a bulb of garlic and presenting it proudly.

I twisted my lips to one side and squinted at him. "Um. What?"

J said his best friend, the one we were about to drive to Montana to see, had advised him to eat a clove or two raw—apparently it was a cure-all, and J was always one for a caper that might result in a story later told.

"So do you swallow it whole, or what?"

"Uh—apparently it only works if I chew it."

He pulled several plump crescents from the bulb and rubbed his thumb across them to remove their paper skins. I watched his eyebrows rise and his eyes bug as he ate two cloves in a row. I couldn't help but laugh.

After a healthy swig of water, J pressed in the clutch and started the engine, released the emergency brake, shifted into first from neutral, and we were on our way. The farther we drove, the more snow. The glass of the passenger seat window felt cold when my head leaned against it. I tried to focus feeling on my right temple, that one point of icy contact. I did not succeed. I said little and cried silently, frustrated by my inability to think of anything other than Emily. Fell in and out of uncomfortable sleep while J drove, fueled by many cups of coffee, a quart of orange juice, a can of sardines from the nook of the car door, a continuous stream of classic rock, and a few pit stops. After nine or ten hours, we arrived in Bozeman.

I knew J's friend and his girlfriend, considered them my friends too. Their hugs were warm, and I was glad to see them. We sat in the kitchen of the house they were renting: walls painted white, a green bowl of pink apples and oranges on the kitchen table. My sadness crowded out every appetite. Still I took off my clothes, still I slept with J, still I ate. The four of us went cross-country skiing, and when I fell flat on my face in the snow, my heart beat fast, but I laughed to make it clear I didn't take my clumsiness too seriously.

We visited Yellowstone National Park. The Rocky Mountains were immense, spotted with snow and buffalo. We stripped down to our underwear, slipped into a natural hot spring; the water carried the scent of sulfur, semi-rotten. Teenagers jumped from tall rocks. I ran from cold snow to hot water, felt my skin stretch across the air.

On our way back to Colorado, J and I stopped for the night in Jackson Hole. A friend of ours was there working with sled dogs; he introduced us to the new litter of puppies: gray fuzz in white snow, chained to wooden poles. A few of the dogs jumped on me when I crouched down to greet them. Their bodies were warm, and I could hear the air move as they breathed. They nipped my nose and my hat, my scarf and my gloves, and I wanted to curl up in their wooden houses and let them chew on the strands of my hair, let them climb all over me. I wanted to hold them. I worried about whether they were warm enough, and happy.

From Wyoming, we headed straight to the campus of our college. Throughout the nine-hour drive, my thoughts kept dragging me to the postcard I'd sent to Emily a few days before she died: whether I'd find it in her dorm room, whether she'd gotten it in time.

When we arrived, I went directly to Emily's residence hall. The sprawling dormitory was over a hundred years old: slate roof above dormer windows, four stories of stone, decorative half-timbering painted forest green, and tall, multipaned glass windows. I entered the building and went to the office of the residential life coordinator, who greeted me with warmth and timidity. I followed her up a flight of stairs, turned left, walked down a wood-paneled hallway, stopped before a door with a corkboard onto which had been pinned a red rose, a wilted daffodil, and five handwritten notes of gratitude. There was, too, a piece of torn cream-colored paper on which Emily had drawn a tiny black fly and the words "You matter."

I remembered, then, the quotes that used to randomly appear on whiteboards in the student center during my senior year, ones like Whitman's line: "To be surrounded

by beautiful, curious, breathing, laughing flesh is enough."
I'd find them and smile, comforted by the handwriting, so
similar to my own, and the knowledge that my little sister
had been there.

The residential life coordinator unlocked the dorm room
door and told me, "Take your time. Just check out at the front
desk before you leave." What lay before me was chaotic. So
much and all in disarray: dried flowers hanging from the ceiling, bookshelves that couldn't contain all their books, straw
baskets full of disposable cameras, orphaned oil pastels and
acrylic paint tubes half used, Bic lighters, and almost-empty
packs of cigarettes. Walls plastered with posters from events
like the Seventh Annual Blackfly Ball (though we'd attended
the eighth) and a print of Henri Matisse's *Dance* and quotes
she liked and cards she'd received and photos: friends and
me and other family, rocks and sprouts and skies, a dog and
the nose of a donkey. Drawings (her own) of nude models
and apple cores. Cutouts of leaves, after Matisse, all over the
place. Empty glass jars and wooden figurines. Shelves made
from cardboard boxes and baking pans. Whisks and ladles
hanging from hooks on the walls and lots of empty beer bottles. The windowsill filled with spider plants, succulents, and
ferns. Some jewelry, little of which I recognized—she must
have given the rest away before she died.

A friend who was the college's current artist in residence
joined me and together we surveyed the space. What to keep
and what to throw away? These impossible decisions were not
mine alone to make, but I'd been given permission to make
them anyway. I think my mother and father both believed
that if the other parent got to Colorado first, he/she might
take pieces of their daughter without an intention to share.
Or maybe it was simpler than that; maybe to imagine dealing
with any of it themselves was too much to bear.

"I don't know what to do with all this shit," I said. So much was clearly the product of a manic high; the rest marked by a low, lonely energy. The postcard was nowhere to be found.

I told my friend to take what she'd like from Emily's art supplies: Prismacolor markers and soft pastel crayons, paint brushes and tubes of heavy body acrylic paint with names like Quinacridone Red, Cadmium Yellow, True Blue. She was hesitant. I insisted. "This all will just sit here otherwise. Please. She would want someone to use them."

An hour or two later—I lost track of time—J appeared with Emily's ginger cat, who'd been kept, kindly and temporarily, by a student who lived off campus. I pulled two glass bottles from the room's minifridge, which was otherwise bare. The three of us sat on the floor in the hallway and shared the beers. The cat's name was Curry. He wore a blue collar with a single silver bell, which rang lamely when he tried to escape beneath our bent legs and tired knees. Maybe he was looking for Emily, or maybe he knew he was flying to New Orleans with me and didn't want to leave.

When we'd finished the bottles, I slipped their mouths around my fingers and waved them over to the small, plastic school-issued trash can in the corner of her room, empty save for a Jimmy John's wrapper and Diet Coke can.

I WENT BACK TO WORK for two weeks and then, when my school's spring break came around in late April, J and I joined his parents on a vacation in the Virgin Islands. It hadn't yet been a full month since Emily died, and I was exhausted. During the flight, I watched the movie *Frozen* for the first time. I thought I could handle something lighthearted. I sobbed at the end, when the spell-breaking true love was revealed to be that between sisters—that which I'd never have again.

The house in which we stayed for five days had a pool overlooking the ocean—every possible shade of blue on blue on blue. I slept on my stomach between polka-dot sheets, one arm dangling off the side of the mattress, the other bent by my face. When I was awake, I took photos with the Nikon camera that I'd taken from my sister's dorm room. I was trying to teach myself how to use it so it wouldn't end up buried in a box in a closet, unused.

J and his parents and I hiked a trail through a forest that led to the brick-and-iron ruins of an old sugar mill—paneless windows, pipes, walls, wheels. Orange-purple legs of hermit crabs, ridged skins of small lizards, thin deer with large ears, gray sticks and dead leaves. At the beach, we tossed striped towels over makeshift thrones of sand. We feasted on sleeves of rice crackers, jars of salsa, slices of white cheese, and salty yellows of hard-boiled eggs. The clouds sat white and indigo above the horizon, hills painted by rocks and leaves yellow green. Sailboats distant and solemn, still and moored. My nail polish was the color of the sea, a turquoise that turned clear at the shoreline. Below the surface of the water, I was weightless, suspended. I spotted a sea turtle and followed him for as long as I could.

J and I had to leave the Virgin Islands two days early to attend a memorial service that the college had organized for Emily. My phone rang while we were at the gate, waiting to board our plane: a friend from college. More accurately, a friend from college whom I slept with during my sophomore year. Even more accurately, a friend from college whom I slept with during my sophomore year, Halloween weekend, when my sixteen-year-old sister was visiting me. That Friday, I'd put on purple Ugg boots, a stretchy striped dress, a red plaid flannel. Emily wore a poofy hot-pink pleather skirt and a rainbow clown-hair wig. My roommate produced from beneath her bed two big bottles of washable paint. We coated our hands with it, then handprinted each other's faces blue and green. Shots, selfies, jack-o'-lanterns, piggyback rides between parties, pee break on the street, fluorescent lights, school cafeteria, plates piled high at midnight with Tater Tots and ketchup, pancakes and syrup. My friends were all pie-eyed and ebullient, and I got to show off my little sister. The next night we went to a dance, and I drunkenly ditched her. Left her to wander campus asking strangers for directions to my apartment.

The friend said, "I heard about your sister—I just wanted to say I'm so sorry." I thanked him for calling, grateful for his bravery. We chatted for a few minutes—where we were in life, what we'd been up to.

Buoyed by the kindness of the call, I sat down in a cushy airport chair next to J and told him about the conversation. J's blue eyes went wide and distant, his face both tense and blank.

I asked, "What?"

He hesitated. One full, silent minute. "Honestly? I'm really angry."

I thought I might have done something wrong. "What do you mean?"

"At Emily. For what she did. To you. Your whole family."

I felt relief wash through my chest. Not only was J not mad at me, but he was angry on my behalf. I hadn't realized that anger directed at someone I love could feel like care. I hadn't realized how much I needed that. I couldn't do it myself. Couldn't let myself. I could be frustrated, annoyed, or upset, but anger had long ago proved itself too dangerous an emotion, too scary. Even if I'd been able to claim anger for myself—to be mad at Emily? For her illness? Absurd, unfair. To say the suicide had done something wrong was the easy story. Still, she'd left me, and now I was stuck here, in this semiplastic chair, waiting, possessed, unable to think of anything more or anything less. I couldn't leave like she did—she'd taken that away. It wasn't fair. Other than the fact that it would destroy my parents, I had no reason to stay.

After nine hours of travel, J and I made it to Denver; I was already drained of all energy when we arrived on our college's campus the next day to join my mother's family in attending the memorial service. (Someone filmed the whole thing for my father and stepmother, who couldn't make it.) Chaplain One—the same man who'd informed me of Emily's death exactly one month before—wore white robes. Chaplain Two wore a black dress beneath a woven multicolored vest. They stood, exposed, before rows of bodies in metal chairs, between two speakers and two giant terra-cotta pots of orange marigolds, purple basil, and Japanese blood grass.

I sat in the way back with J, in the grass, in a floppy straw hat and flip-flops and a dress that had been Emily's. It would've been easy for someone to mistake me for my sister if she weren't dead and we weren't all here to do arts and crafts in her memory.

Chaplain Two was first to speak. "I invite you in your own way to take a moment to bring yourself to this place."

The moment was filled by sun, bare tree branches, wind. In the front row, my mother stared at a blade of grass just past her feet. On either side of her: the white-blond hair of my fourteen-year-old half sibling, Ches, and the ball cap worn by my stepfather. A few seats down, the president of the college crossed her legs and sighed. In the next row back were seated Bubbie, in a yellow-and-black jacket, and my stepfamily: my grandparents and my aunt and uncle and two of their three kids, all of whom live in Colorado.

"We gather in the beauty of this space by the college's farm, a place that Emily loved, to honor her and celebrate a passionate, deeply creative woman whose friendship enriched all of our lives. We gather today to give gratitude for Emily, who even in the struggles of her own life gifted us with generosity and compassion. And a special sense of belonging that brought us together in real ways, calling us to be a community where there is space for each of us to speak and share the truth of our lives, and begin our own healing."

The school's president told a stilted story of how, during her weekly office hours in the student center, Emily would often share ideas with her. "But before she launched into anything, she always asked how I was, how my kids were." Pearls around her neck, the president looked out at the crowd, past my mother, and returned to her seat. *How are your children?* The question hung in the air like a slash, a hiss, something leaked.

A student spoke next, fumbled syntax, said, "Sorry, I'm nervous and also sad right now." She read "The Peace of Wild Things," a poem by Wendell Berry, and her voice broke at the penultimate line: *and I feel above me the day-blind stars*. People clapped, though it wasn't a performance. Ches brought their eyes down to their hands—their body slouched impressively. My mother placed an arm on their back. My stepfather unclasped his hands and placed one of them on my mother's left thigh.

Emily's friend Z, the one who'd called me the day of in a panic, sang a Regina Spektor song and played guitar with another student as they sat in folding chairs. Their voices were warm and thin and shaky. Ches again buried their head in their hands; my mother rubbed their shoulder. The college president wiped her eyes.

Chaplain Two spoke again. "Her pain was something that though she shared it with others, she also kept it close to herself. We didn't see all of Emily, and this makes Emily's death harder. We will never fully know why. We can guess, try to piece things together, but we will never know. Perhaps our task for the moment is accepting and voicing our emotions."

We were instructed to each write a small prayer or gratitude on a construction paper leaf, then hang the leaf on a young tree, front and center. Bluegrass music played. I watched as others placed loops of yarn on tender branches: members of my family; a girl in a black hoodie with a butterfly on the back, who'd taken care of Emily's cat after her death; the residents of the hall for which Emily was a residential advisor during her sophomore year; boys in tank tops beneath flannels; girls in flowy skirts or overalls. I felt unsure of what to write. I did not feel particularly grateful; I had no small prayers. I was afraid to reveal anything.

When I finally walked up to the tree, my stepfather stood. I hung my leaf, turned around, bent down, kissed my mother, let my stepfather hug me. J was by my side. He wore a brown felt hat. I didn't wait for him. I almost ran back. The construction paper leaves fluttered, all different colors— yellow, orange, green, blue, purple, red, pink. I hated how normal the scene seemed.

Chaplain One said, "When the wind blows, the prayers get said over and over again." He talked about gratitude and then prayed that we would all find our way—would "experience the goodness of life and find the gentleness of spirits, even in our darkest, most confusing moments." Then he invited everyone to eat brick-oven pizza and to finger paint.

AT THE CONCLUSION OF SPRING BREAK, I returned to New Orleans to finish out the school year. I came into work late and left early for the last three days of April and the entirety of May. I had no focus or motivation and was getting very little sleep. I worried I would be reprimanded, yet was unable to wake up when my alarm went off, couldn't make myself stay till the last school bell rang. Though I'm sure it didn't go unnoticed, no one ever mentioned it to me.

Each evening was a painful string of hours by myself in my house. From Emily's dorm room I'd taken a gray shirt that smelled like her skin, an oversized Jazz Fest T-shirt that our aunt and uncle had given her fifteen years earlier, plus her cowboy boots and a pair of light-blue Converse low-top sneakers that were identical to mine. Her MacBook Pro too. More often than not, I'd put on one of the shirts and the cowboy boots and pace the kitchen, then sit down on the couch. TV on to fill the silence, the cat doing whatever he pleased. I'd open up the laptop, type in her password (which I'd correctly guessed), and wait as the device warmed to life. It was the only source of anything that passed as a clue: blue digital folders containing photos she'd taken and papers she'd written for school, all her music, websites she'd visited, her search history.

It was from reading through Emily's emails in those weeks that I learned about the poison, how long she'd had a plan: three weeks after I forwarded her a quote I thought she'd like, one week before she arrived in New Orleans, and fifteen minutes before we G Chat-ed casually, she received an email from an online store confirming her purchase of twenty bottles of lime sulfur for $337. I gathered details like the exact time she'd placed the order for the dinner she ate on the night of her death (3:37 p.m.) and that after March 23 she'd stopped reading her emails. Perhaps it was no wonder I couldn't fall asleep. Today when I hear someone's iPhone ring with the same tone that I snoozed and snoozed and snoozed and snoozed and snoozed through on those mornings, I still shrink.

A couple of weeks after Emily died, I'd found a therapist by googling *grief + eating disorder + therapist + new orleans*. When she asked what I'd been doing to cope with the loss, I told her that my friend AJ had mailed me a pair of yoga pants and a new journal, which I'd been writing in regularly. My therapist suggested painting and tuning in to my body.

On a Saturday morning in late May, I sat on my porch in the sun, dipped my fingers into cool paint, and wiped them across smooth white paper; stiffness in my back, a knot taking over my chest, my eyes wet, my belly soft and somersaulting. There was no space. I stood, rinsed off my hands, grabbed my iPad, and began to walk toward the bayou. I stopped in a coffee shop, took my plastic cup across the street to a triangle-shaped patch of green formed by the intersection of Grand Route Saint John and Mystery Streets with Esplanade Avenue. Sat down on a metal bench amid elephant ears and cast-iron plants, the shade of palmettos. Nearby, pairs of men played chess side by side on stone tables trimmed with mosaic tiles.

I took a sip of the iced coffee, tapped my tablet awake, and opened up the Notes app. I typed without thinking, without stopping. What came out surprised me. I knew I was "grieving," but I hadn't known what had been eating away at me. ("I'm driving over the Claiborne Avenue Bridge and I can't call my sister just to talk or for any other reason because she's dead. Is that real? Or am I imagining it like I did during those other drives when I was distracted by the possibility that my sister might one day kill herself?"; "I feel like I should be crying but instead, most of the time, I'm moving on with my life and both fearing and hoping each day that the memories will fade and, with them, both the joy and the pain of having Emily as my sister. My sister who is [am I supposed to say 'was'?] the person I loved the most in the entire world.") And now that I knew, I wanted someone else to know, too, and my sister had already killed herself, and nothing worse could possibly happen to me—the hurt was so deep it took the form of invulnerability. On May 26 I edited what I'd written, gave it the title "It's Been Two Months," and published it online on Medium. Though I wasn't sure it was appropriate, I shared a link to the post on Facebook.

Within one week, over five thousand people read those 902 words. I felt exposed and relieved, proud and terrified; I held on for dear life to the connection, the attention, the validation, the ability to be honest and to be heard. I resolved to continue to write in my journal, and then, once another month had passed, to share again.

For five years, I chronicled my grief. Much of that writing is in these pages. It is how this book began.

JUNE ARRIVED, AND MY MOTHER flew down to help me pack up my house. We folded clothes into duffel bags and books into boxes. I asked JK to hold on to the oversized items that I intended to come back for eventually: my bicycle, which was light blue; the desk I'd bought when all I knew about teaching was that I'd need a desk; the charcoal grill/ smoker I'd gifted J from a secondhand store on Elysian Fields Avenue. The rest of the furniture I gave away, save for a serious, sturdy wood chair that Emily and I picked out together in a Bywater vintage shop—that went into the back seat of my ten-year-old white Passat. When the house was empty and the car completely full, my mother returned home, and I flew, again, to Colorado.

J and I went backpacking in the Flat Tops Wilderness Area with our chocolate lab / bully breed mix. For three days, the clouds were impeccable and the sky stayed blue. The trail of red-brown dirt we hiked was surrounded by knobby white aspens; into one trunk, J carved our initials with the edge of a knife. I was so tired. The act seemed delusional, desperate— romantic gesture as antidote to misery.

On the last day, we paused in a spot of shade, took off our packs. My hair was greasy. The air was dry and the sun was strong. I cupped my hand over the mouth of my Nalgene and tipped it to one side to create a stream from which the dog could drink. J sat down on a rock. I envied the ease with which he seemed to be existing. So burden-free. He didn't understand, he'd never understand, how grief pinned me, its weight not quite crushing because the crushing would be nice—to be flattened would provide a relief on the border of pleasure. In the distance was a tree with broad, bright green leaves, almost pulsing. I did not blink.

"What's wrong?"

"What do you mean, 'What's wrong'?" I said. My vision had started to blur. Then I turned to J, looked him dead in the eye. "You're really asking me that? What do you *think* is wrong?"

"I'm sorry— It just seemed like you were okay and then all of a sudden you weren't . . ."

"How do you not get this? Do you actually think I'm not thinking about Emily literally all of the time? I don't get breaks. It doesn't go away."

"Okay. I know."

"No, you don't know!"

I took a deep breath, looked up at the sky.

"That's the whole problem: you don't know," I said. "You don't get it. You can't. You never will."

"I'm sorry, baby. It's not going to be like this forever. It won't always be this hard." He was trying to be nice. I didn't let him.

"That's not true. It doesn't change! It doesn't change. My sister is dead. I'm always going to be thinking about her. It's never going to be okay." I was not exaggerating. I believed what I was saying. I couldn't imagine being anything other than devastated and alone. Then I couldn't catch my breath. I stood gasping. Beside me, J instructed, "Breathe. Breathe. Breathe."

WHILE I WAS WITH J, my car sat for a week in the Southern summer sun, fully packed. I returned to a trunk perfumed with melted candle wax and drove east on I-10, then north via I-65, 85, and 95. I didn't have much of a plan except to join my mother, stepfather, and Ches, all of whom were on their respective summer breaks, at Bubbie's beach house in New Jersey.

When I arrived, I found my mother in bed with her iPad. This was where she stayed, somewhere between asleep and awake. Sometimes she'd join the rest of us for a meal; sometimes she could eat. The mother I knew spent whole days reading novels—this version could not focus on a single page.

On the outside, my stepfather, Ches, Bubbie, and I appeared alive while we rotted away inside. We grilled sweet corn on the deck and sliced through plums with dull knives. My stepfather made pots of oatmeal for anyone to eat, waited for the wind to pick up, and asked, "Who wants to go sailing!" More often than not, he tacked his twenty-year-old Hobie Cat across the bay alone. Ches went to the beach with their friends, played video games, and demolished bowls of Honey Nut Cheerios and boxes of Kraft Mac & Cheese. In the mornings, Bubbie sat at the kitchen table in her pajamas and read the newspaper. She drank one cup of coffee and ate one slice of peanut butter toast with one half of a banana. At night, movies continued to play on the TV in her room long after she'd fallen asleep.

I tried to read books, scroll through pictures and posts, eat cherries and spit out their pits, swim laps in the bay, go on runs. I tried to watch the new season of *Orange Is the New Black*. I was trying to be twenty-four. I was trying to tire myself out so that I could fall asleep at night. I tried to think about nothing. Took walks along the ocean. Tried to focus on the blueness of the sky and the shapes of the clouds and the burn of the sun and the sand on my skin.

Instead, I listed names I might give to children I didn't have. Thought about wanting to have children just so I could name them after my dead sister. Wondered if it was a twisted thought. Perhaps one my mother had also had; my middle and Hebrew names are after her own dead sister, after all. I couldn't imagine myself, like her, pregnant at twenty-four.

My own twenty-fourth birthday had come just shy of three weeks after Emily died. It was the first night of Passover, and it was raining hard. I attended a seder in a garage, its door open to the sound of steady downpour. Across from me were seated two sisters. I asked polite questions—what they did, where they were from. Their answers revealed a pattern of language so established and intimate that my shoulders stiffened to stem the jealousy. I excused myself to the restroom, a cramped space in which I stood and watched myself cry in the mirror, surrounded by red-and-gold wallpaper. Used the toilet paper to wipe my eyes.

I was exhausted when I got home. I called J. He sounded cheerful. He was busy setting the table for his own seder in Colorado. I tried to keep things light, but I felt heavy. I ended the call. I could not ask for what I wanted because I didn't know what I wanted, beyond wanting him to know what I wanted without either of us having to ask.

I got into bed to go to sleep, but my mind began to create a list woven from things to do, things not to do, things I should and shouldn't have done. The result was less list, more continual sense that everything I said and felt and did was wrong. I slept, eventually. Until something registered in my drowsy consciousness as sudden, unexpected, and loud, and I startled myself awake with my own involuntary scream. I didn't know what had happened. I was afraid that a stranger was in the house with me. I waited, unmoving, in the dark to hear another sound. I didn't know how much time had passed. When I was able to make myself turn on a light, I saw on the floor a frame that had fallen from my bedroom wall: beneath cracked and broken glass was a cyanotype Emily had made for me.

In mid-July, I left the beach to spend time with my father and stepmother at their house in Pennsylvania: a two-story colonial with hardwood floors, built in 1930, painted white with indigo-blue shutters. Our father moved there when Emily was six and I was nine. It was far from our swim meets and play rehearsals and softball practices and Sunday school classes in Delaware. It was far from all our friends.

The weekends we spent there were a balancing act of trying to avoid upsetting our father and trying to avoid being bored. He and our stepmother played games with us: Boggle, Mastermind for Kids, Splash!, Wise and Otherwise, *Mario Party* for Nintendo 64. We were taken to fencing classes and drum lessons, though neither stuck. I often wandered into the kitchen and scrubbed the stacks of dishes in the sink or scraped sticky rings of soy sauce and jelly from the refrigerator shelves. Sometimes Emily and I took a trip to the public library by ourselves.

We did this, too, in Delaware. We were voracious readers, and in both places the walk was but a few blocks. I loved books by Roald Dahl, Lois Lowry, and E. L. Konigsburg; Emily liked all those, too, plus Philip Pullman's His Dark Materials books and Lemony Snicket's A Series of Unfortunate Events. We brought novels to dinner and tried to get away with reading under the table. After being tucked into bed at our mother's house, I'd continue to read by the very dim light of a digital clock so that I wouldn't get caught.

At our father's house we stayed up late watching Disney Channel original movies or reruns of The Brady Bunch on Nick at Nite and eating junk food—Drake's cakes, Entenmann's doughnuts, Bugles from our fingertips, cheese puffs. One summer night, past midnight, there was nothing worth watching and Emily was flipping through the channels too slowly. I was fourteen and wanted the remote and my eleven-year-old sister wouldn't give it to me. She was stubborn and I was stubborn. She ignored my demands until I got up from my seat on the cracking ivory leather couch, took the thin flesh of her forearm in my hands, and began to twist. She tried not to yield—I watched her face twist with me, big brown eyes and their lashes turning hard and cold, turning terrified in the same way mine had when my father wrestled the remote from my clenched fist.

From the time I was old enough to drive the thirteen miles between our parents' houses by myself, Emily and I did what we could to keep time with our father confined to a lunch or a dinner, maybe a movie in a theater. We preferred to stay clear of the sweep of his anger. We preferred any activity with him to have a set beginning and end so it would be clear when the visit was over, so we could flee the hurt of wanting to leave our father who only wanted his daughters to stay.

I'm not sure whether I agreed to a longer stay at my father's house that summer out of love or pity or a sense of obligation. (I'm not sure whether they can be distinguished.) I thought I might be there for a week. I only lasted three nights.

J was away, so our dog was with me. While making myself lunch on day four, I put an empty yogurt container on the kitchen floor for her to lick clean. My father's dog entered the room, my dog growled, and the barking began. My father ran into the room yelling at the animals and/or me. He picked up a foot and swung it toward a body. Reflexively, I called out, "Don't touch my dog!"

"Becca, relax." It could have been nice, end of scene. But it wasn't—it was loud and berating, so I said something back, which became an argument, which exploded. It happened so fast: I tried to walk away, but he grabbed me by my right wrist, kept me there, and when I said "Let go of me" repeatedly, he didn't listen, so I did the only thing I could in the moment, I didn't think at all; I broke the dinner plate in my left hand over his bald head and the blow shocked us both. He let go. I bolted up the stairs. Gathered all my things, left the house shaking while he yelled from the wide-open front door. I walked down the street with my dog on her leash and a heavy duffel bag strapped across my body. It was hot and sunny. I sweated while I cried. My phone battery was at 12 percent, and as I called different people who might be able to come pick me up, I was panicked it would die.

I HAD TO GET AWAY FROM THE CHAOS OF MY FAMILY, so I lived out the remainder of the summer in J's parents' basement in the suburbs of Philly, joining them in the evenings to eat dinner and then watch *The Daily Show*. They took care of me unquestioningly and, in the fall, let me and J stay in their second home in Maine.

I told myself and those around me that I was going to use this unstructured time to study for the GRE; I had a vague notion of attending graduate school eventually. Instead, I spent the first few weeks of September on a couch watching movies and waiting, almost praying, for time to pass. I couldn't make myself move except to get water or food and to go for a mile-long run. I couldn't always manage even that. I relished the end of each day: the sun's setting rays as they made their way toward the lapping bay, casting in gold the black-eyed Susans and tall white pines, the lobster traps and tangled seaweed.

I decided I needed to be occupied. I began by baking: sticky cinnamon buns and pumpkin cranberry muffins, pretzels and pizza dough. I wrote in my journal, or in letters to friends. A few chilly mornings, I filled a thermos with hot coffee, got into a kayak, and paddled out onto the still bay. Went on long bike rides with J through a forest of fir, spruce, birch, and maple trees. Came closer to checking off the six-month-old box beside *Finish sending funeral thank-you notes*. I got myself a job as a nanny for two young boys. It felt good to work again, to be busy. School pickups and drop-offs gave me a different way to mark the time—a way that depended less on how long it had been since my sister died and more on tending to two little lives.

There were, too, future plans: J and I had decided to travel together internationally for as long as we could—until we ran out of patience and/or had drained our small savings accounts. He would quit his job and we would leave on the first of December for Thailand, where we'd arranged to work on a chicken farm in exchange for room and board. We used credit card points and airline miles to buy tickets from Newark to Chiang Mai, from Bangkok to Sydney; we made hostel reservations and applied for visas; we went to a travel medicine clinic to get vaccines and prescriptions for malaria pills; we started a travel blog on Tumblr and sent messages to potential WWOOF host sites; we bought first aid kit supplies.

I was trying so hard to be okay that there were hours, even days, when it didn't feel like something was wrong. Still, there were moments in between all the doing, quiet ones, that took me to a pinhole that siphoned air from my lungs. Once, this occurred while I lay in the bath: face up, ears underwater, eyes fixed on the cream-colored ceiling. The rising steam thick but clean. Breath slow and measured, with the distant resonance of an astronaut or scuba diver. My mind turned to black boxes. The passengers on the Malaysia Airlines plane that disappeared nearly three weeks before my sister. It occurred to me then that a detailed log of anything's final hours is the kind of thing you only think you want to have, the kind of thing you only think will help you determine what went wrong. The possibility of such a record might tease out of you the same sort of obsession you might have over details after learning that someone has cheated on you. The unshakably gut-wrenching need to get answers by searching twenty-three thousand square miles of the southern Indian Ocean, by asking who-what-where-how when all you really want to know is why. The fixation on the time leading up to the end as a cushion—a way to soften the slap of never really knowing what you're really wondering: What could I have done differently? And: Did you think about how much it would hurt me (when you disappeared)?

I stepped out of the tub. Wrapped a towel round my body and walked dripping straight to the bed. Curled wet knees to chest beneath thick covers. Through a window I could see the edges of the clouds were a tender pinkish gray. Old, mellow music wafted up from the first floor. I was so tired of dragging my sunken heart around. I lay in bed, waiting for J. It was dark by the time he opened the door to the bedroom. His entrance was tentative, delicate. Very softly, he said, "Hey."

I knew if I answered, I might say something unkind. I pretended not to hear.

Perhaps he felt hurt, frustrated, unsure of what to do anymore. I don't know what was said, what happened next. The memory becomes clear again in the moment when I am sobbing in the dark, when my bare body shakes almost violently, when I know I've been cruel and impossible to please and I say, "You should be with someone better," and he says, "There is no one better," and then I tell him again and again that cannot be true because even my sister left me, she left me, even she left me.

PART 2

Dear M&M's,

This is the nickname that I have so affectionately given myself (and you, I guess) in sixth grade. I wonder if I (rather, you) still think about "small" things like sixth grade. My life doesn't seem insignificant now, but as you struggle to remember what sixth grade was like, you are probably thinking that life was uncomplicated. It doesn't seem like it is now, so maybe I'll set a few things straight.

My friends are a huge part of my life, and I wonder: Is it still like that? Each day I share my loud, animated laugh (Is it still that bad?) with them. It's hard to imagine not being with my BFFs (best friends forever, in case our "cool" terms are forgotten), but I can only guess that you're no longer close with them. What happened? I guess your life is the consequences of my choices now, and I can only hope that I didn't screw us up badly, in terms of friendships, my family, school, etc.

My family is pretty typical. We fight, make up, hug, and then continue our daily routines. As I sit here and reflect upon them, I can't believe it! When you get this letter, Becca will be turning twenty-one! She already seems mature and ready for the world. I mean, I always knew she was "old," but the thought scares me. Does that seem old to you, being the grown-up eighteen-year-old that you are? Ches just turned five and is still singing the Spider-Man theme song and changing costumes every two minutes (with the exception of dinner, where they're forced to sit still). [Stepdad] and Mom are exasperating sometimes, and I hope I'm more independent by eighteen. (They can still pay for college though.) Dad and I are beginning to work things out. We used to get in a lot of fights (which I would find hard for you to forget, because they could be considerably frightening), but things are beginning to cool down.

School isn't that bad. I hope that all of my schoolwork and extracurricular activities have benefited you in some way or another. With field hockey, trumpet, Hebrew school, drama club, etc., sometimes I don't know how to handle it. How much has my life changed? Are you still a hectic, busy person? More importantly, have you fulfilled any of the goals that I've set for myself?

The only way I can remind you of my current important values is to lecture you about them now: Appreciate the little things in life, and ALWAYS laugh at inside jokes. Study hard (and I hope that you and I didn't bomb the rest of the Word of the Day tests), but never let school overwhelm you. IT'S NOT THE ONLY IMPORTANT THING! Even though we'll be off to college soon, we've both worked hard (or up until I know, anyway), and you deserve some time off once in a while. But that doesn't mean you should drink excessively, smoke, or do anything reckless without consulting your inner sixth-grade soul. I don't know everything, but I know that it will only be for the best!

If we still share the same interests and goals, you'll be going off to college to be a teacher, marine biologist, actress, professor studying synesthesia, and author. But do our soon-to-be-exhausted life a favor and pick one, please! Your body and my soul will be traveling around the world, seeing the sights and laughing away time. Oh, and as far as eating, keep up my vegetarian standards. It means a lot to me, seeing as our environment is worsening. Even though I already know it's a pain to get the right amount of protein, I hope you have stuck with it. I stood up to the people who questioned my choice, so I'm depending on you to prove them wrong.

Right now I have very specific favorites. I love the colors sky blue, neon green, lilac purple, and black. My room is sky blue with clouds and a cloud-covered bed, and it makes me feel as if I'm floating away in my own world. I love to listen to Pink Floyd, U2, the Beatles, Rush, Led Zeppelin, etc. They may not be the hottest bands of our generation, but I couldn't care less. After all, what's the point of listening to something that is popular but that you don't even like? I would be shocked if you aren't crazy about *Calvin and Hobbes*. There's something about it that is irresistible, no matter what age. I hate tomatoes, mushrooms, and pink. Mom says that I'll learn to like them. I doubt it, but I guess I'll give it a chance someday. I know that some of my likes and dislikes will change, but won't I always be in the back of your mind reminding you how much you hated pink, yet loved Pink Floyd?

Overall, I hope you're doing well. This is written for an English assignment and a grade, but it is really meant to remind you of the immature sixth grade M&M's that still lives inside you. Wherever this may find you, I hope it finds you well and in good health.

From the little part of your conscience,

(m) + (m)'s /a.k.a Emily

I KNEW WHAT WAS GOING ON BEFORE our parents did: I was fifteen with braces and Emily was twelve with thick brown hair down the length of her back. It was the summer after ninth/sixth grade. Maybe I had been reading her journal again or maybe it was because she'd stopped eating ketchup straight from the packet and I'd been a girl in middle school once too: the eyeliner and mascara, the skin-tight sparkly camisoles, how we all starved and shaved our changing bodies.

We were on a trip to London with our grandparents—the first time either of us had left the country. For lunch one afternoon we stepped into Wagamama, a hip Japanese noodle bar chain. The portions were generous, warm, and salty. Our grandparents laughed at how quickly Emily slurped up her yasai yaki soba noodles—like a puppy eating from a bowl. She smiled with empty eyes, then excused herself to the bathroom with too much honey in her voice. I waited a minute—less—then followed. I bent over and peeked under the stalls on a hunch that I'd see feet facing the wrong direction and that they'd be hers. I called her name out as a question because I knew she wouldn't throw up if she knew I was there.

We spoke about it once, six or seven years afterward. She asked me how I'd known, and I said probably the same way she did—we were sisters. During one of those winter break dinners when I was home from college, I'd excused myself from the dining room table at our mother's house and stayed away a bit too long. When I emerged, Emily was standing in the hallway between the kitchen and the bathroom, right next to a framed collage Bubbie had made from our old socks. She asked, "Are you okay? Were you throwing up?" and I gave her a look like she was wrong.

At our father's house that fall, Emily's behavior was not particularly worrisome—not the midnight runs, not the careful consumption of half a veggie burger with just mustard, not the commitment to drinking water nor the blades of her shoulders, not the four days she went without eating anything except Tums nor the pro-anorexia websites she spent hours on.

At our mother's house, I'd stand in my socks on the blue kitchen countertops, opening cabinet doors in search of something sweet. It had all been hidden from Emily. The marshmallows lived in an empty coffee bean can, the maple syrup behind a plastic crate filled with tea. In her room she hid the wrappers of food she binged: under pillows, in her sock drawer, beneath big piles of books or bigger piles of dirty laundry. During dinner, she'd sit at the table for hours, determined not to take the bite she needed to take for permission to leave.

It must have been strange to be treated as sick in one place and fine in another. Was the pathology real or imagined? By the end of April, when Emily starred as Audrey in a middle school production of *Little Shop of Horrors*, she was so skinny it was scary—a smudge of a person once there. From my seat in the audience I watched her move across the stage in a lacy black cocktail dress with spaghetti straps, mesmerized by the fullness and strength of her voice, and also by the thinness of her arms and legs and torso. I wished I could be more like her.

(At first I remembered her costume as a dress of mine that she'd borrowed, then realized I was the one who had borrowed it from her to wear to my eleventh-grade home-coming dance. It was too big on her, and very tight on me.)

By then, she was already six weeks into treatment for an eating disorder, coverage for which our stepfather was per-petually fighting with insurance companies: the appoint-ments with psychologists, psychiatrists, nutritionists; an outpatient eating disorder treatment program an hour away that she attended three-to-five days a week for two months; an outpatient integrated behavioral health program in Philadelphia. Plus twice-weekly therapy (individual and family), a diagnosis of severe depression and medication to match, and a mandate to eat a set number of calories each day. Each morning before school our stepfather made my thirteen-year-old sister scrambled eggs, whole wheat toast with precisely measured pats of butter, and a glass of milk or orange juice. She forced herself to eat as much of it as she could bear while I hurried out the door to get to my first period concert band class with maybe a handful of Cheerios in a plastic sandwich bag.

I don't remember talking about it with friends—how my sister wasn't eating, how she cut what was left of the flesh on her upper left arm—even though we'd all known one another for at least six years by the time we were in tenth grade. My English teacher that year was new and nervous—mousy in every clichéd sense of the word, her glasses funny black rectangles on her long, freckled face. She made us read poems we didn't understand and spoke to us like we were children, was far too nice when we mis-behaved. But she dressed cute and her eyes were pretty, so we knew there was hope for her. When I had to write a five-page research paper for her class on how museums lay claim to artifacts, I missed an assignment deadline. My tears sur-prised me when I pulled the teacher aside after class and said the words aloud for the first time, thinking they were more excuse than truth: "My sister is really sick. It's all I can think about. I can't focus."

It was only after Emily died that I learned how and when her eating disorder began. The discovery was accidental: I was looking through her email account for something else when I spotted a message addressed to the director of our college's writing center. Attached was a literacy narrative she'd been assigned to write as part of her training to become a peer tutor:

> Literacy was dangerous for me. Not initially, of course—innocently enough, my first word was "book." Listening to my mother read aloud, I memorized and recited the words of *Where the Wild Things Are*, progressing along the expected track of early childhood until I could read on my own. I devoured the Magic Tree House series, and my cravings were satisfied by whatever was stacked around the house. There was plenty: my sister and I had more books than toys. I developed a suddenly insatiable appetite for *Calvin and Hobbes*; I read and bought the entire collection, including the three that were only published in Puerto Rico. This hunger became borderline obsessive—I could recite any strip, stayed up late singing Hobbes's favorite word, "smock," in a voice that I thought only for my audience until my parents' yells of "Go to bed!" from their room below proved otherwise.
>
> I realize now that the words I read, I adopted as organic tattoos, their ink seeping into my very being. This didn't matter much as long as I was reading *The Hobbit*, there was only so long I could pretend to have hairy feet and a sense of heroic purpose, but my book selection was random and at whim. I picked books for the authors I

liked. Books for their weight in my hands. Books for their color. And with the shockingly pink cover of a book I picked on a family road trip to Detroit, literacy was no longer a normative pursuit. In an unassuming Barnes & Noble on an otherwise unremarkable day, my literacy became a precarious guidebook.

This pink cover was *Perfect*, perfectly normal, the preteen story of Isabelle Lee navigating a dysfunctional family, the discovery of a coping mechanism, an eventual happy ending. Isabelle Lee had an eating disorder, and my twelve years of literary embodiment told me that these words were worth exploring.

I remember very little of the next two years of my life, but I do know that the escapism that books had faithfully provided became an unvarnished dedication to building myself an eating disorder. My memories rest not in the hospitals my ninety-pound body was sanctioned to, but in *Wasted*, an unremitting memoir of an adult woman's eating disorder. The book became my bible, my instruction manual; my voracious appetite for books became a restricted denial of any hunger at all. I underlined and earmarked my newfound guide: What were the best ways to starve myself? To manipulate my family into believing I was eating? How could I align my mind with Marya Hornbacher's, who had so successfully created an existence that would ease my own?

Even my writing became a tool of starvation—I chronicled my successful weight loss, chastised dreaded binges, degraded imperfections. I was trapped in a vocabulary of disease. But as all books end and ink dries, so, too, did the safety in my eating disorder; my family knew, I was tired of hospitals, and recovery was looming. I oscillated between the clean pages of eating disorder accounts— thinspiration, so to speak—and the real world. And so my chosen consecration in *Wasted* became a reluctant *Life Without Ed*. With a painfully slow commitment to recovery, I learned to use the same personification of words that triggered my entrapment to release me from it.

Today my feet are planted solidly in the real world, eating disorder–free, but my literacy will forever be defined by my tendency to internalize what I read and to embed my life in what I write. I now seek nourishment from what I read; I scribble exclamation points in book margins aside great, big, beautiful ideas about the world that make my heart skip.

THE FIRST TIME EMILY TRIED to kill herself was three years into her recovery. It was early April—the air neither warm nor cool. Public school students in Delaware were on spring break and Emily was on her way to a party. It's almost banal: a high school classmate's parents are out of town and there's nothing else to do around here anyway. The moon is waning and the house is full. There's alcohol everywhere and teenagers down-ing it, free for a night and instantly that much older, playing parts they've picked up from the movies. Emily chooses the role of the drunk, jealous seventeen-year-old who catches her ex-boyfriend (who she might still probably love) kissing another girl. She slaps him, then walks away, then returns and bangs on the second-floor bathroom door. "Let me in / we need to talk / let me in / so we can talk / let me in / I'm not going away." When he opens the door, she sits down on the floor and, for several hours, that's where they stay.

The ex wakes up to the sound of light rain. He sees Emily a few feet away, the legion of faint white lines on her left arm in motion, at work: she is push-twisting the childproof cap on a bottle of pills. Maybe she is hungover. Maybe she is still drunk. Maybe they passed out before the conversation could end well. He knows that she is ill. He grabs the bottle from her hands, but she already has a fistful of aspirin. He grabs her wrist and she freezes. He uses his phone to call another party attendee—a friend of both mine and Emily's. She is in her own bed just three houses down the street. He says, "Please come quickly." It doesn't take long. She is gentle when she asks Emily, "What's wrong?" Emily says nothing. The ex and the friend struggle to unclench her fist, flush the pills down the toilet. By then, the sun is out—a new day.

Emily says she is going to go downstairs, and our friend says, "I'll come with you." Then Emily bolts. Instead of running straight out the front door she turns left toward the smell of a mess. She sees half-empty cans of beer and bottles of Smirnoff covering the countertops. She sees cheese puff dust and potato chip crush. She sees knives in a wooden block and pulls out the biggest one. Blade to neck by the time our friend catches up; her scream is both metal and ice. Emily won't let go; they go to the ground. The friend pins Emily down and the ex enters the scene just in time: he takes away the knife.

The girl whose home this has all taken place in begs them not to call 911—she will get in so much trouble if her parents find out there was alcohol at the party—but our friend makes the call anyway. She then calls our mother, who is visiting her own mother in Florida. Our mother calls our stepfather. The police are already there when he arrives. Emily is a pile of sobs. Can't or won't talk, can't or won't walk. They want to take her to a local hospital. Our stepfather runs over and promises he'll take Emily to inpatient himself, then scoops her up and buckles her into his truck. The police follow. He drives calmly as ever, obeying traffic signs and speed limits. He is terrified, convinced that Emily will try to open the door and throw herself from the car.

As Emily is being admitted to the hospital, I am two time zones west, eating a bowl of Cheerios before my nine o'clock class. When my phone rings, I see our friend's name and assume she herself is in crisis. The cell service is poor in the college cafeteria, and late '90s pop music is playing from the speakers overhead, and when I pick up I hear our friend hyperventilating between words and tears.

"Hello? I'm sorry—I can hardly hear you," I say. I walk across the room, circumnavigating tables to try to find a pinprick of reception. "Emily tried to stab herself . . . I called 911 . . . your stepdad . . . hospital . . . don't know . . . fault . . . sorry . . ."

I miss most of what she says, but I know enough to know that something has gone wrong. I tell her it's not her fault, it's going to be okay. I don't know what else to say. I leave the dining hall and walk straight to class. My sister spends a week in an adolescent inpatient program at a behavioral health hospital, without shoelaces, bobby pins, makeup, erasers, or underwire bras.

The day after Emily was discharged, I turned twenty. I asked for a plane ticket for my birthday. I flew home to see her the day after that. We spent the weekend eating bowls of frozen berries with our fingers, watching episodes of *Project Runway*, and talking. Emily described her stay with her signature dramatic flair.

"My bed was so stiff, and my roommate was annoying as hell, and my head always hurt—there was usually at least one person in the hall screaming. But actually the other patients were what kept things interesting—there was a little kid with the worst ADD, two people that hear voices, a guy that stabbed his mom, and a whole bunch of people with suicide attempts."

"What did you *do* there? Did they make you go to group therapy or anything?"

"It was super structured. The nurses watched us all the time, and there were a lot of activities that we were required to participate in, like group therapy and art therapy and individual therapy, plus meal times. All of it was stupid and pretty much sucked, but at least I was occupied. When there

was down time I was desperate for something that would
help keep my mind off things, something to hold on to.
Mostly I wrote or sketched in my journal."

"You had your journal with you?"

"Yeah—on the first day, after [Stepdad] dropped me off,
he went back home to get some of my stuff for me and I
asked him to grab it. I was allowed to have the journal—I just
couldn't write or draw in pen or pencil because, you know,
I might hurt myself with it." She rolled her eyes. "But thank
god I had that—it was intensely liberating just to be able
to create in my journal, something completely and totally
my own. And calming too. Instead of thinking, I was just
doing—getting out the depression and anxiety."

DURING THE SPRING SEMESTER of my last year of college, anxiety about my impending adult life had me awake most nights at three or four o'clock. I was running a lot on my own and drinking a lot with my friends and, in between, I ate little more than raw almonds and air-popped popcorn. Emily was in her first year at the same school. I took comfort in her presence, and I loved being the cool senior in the eyes of all her freshman friends. I was also glad to have an eye on her, to make sure she was okay. Each week for therapy—and also when she was late on refilling her scripts and ran out of meds and also when she wanted to buy a purple jumpsuit from the local thrift store— she'd ask to borrow my car, an old gold Toyota Camry that our mother's parents had handed down to me.

Each week we met by the entrance to the dining hall in the student center; she used her meal plan to swipe me in for a Meatless Monday dinner. We piled high plastic blue plates with greens or noodles. For dessert, we ate bowls of cereal and palmed pieces of fruit that we slid into our backpacks— oranges, peaches, apples. Some Friday nights, in place of getting drunk at house parties, Emily would come over to my house off campus, where I lived with four boys. We'd lie on my full mattress on the floor and watch TV shows on my laptop (mostly *30 Rock* or *Scrubs*). She'd spend the night and steal the covers; I'd talk in my sleep.

One Sunday in the middle of February, cold and sunny, Emily kept me company while I chopped onions and carrots for a curry that I planned to bring to a boy I liked, J, and his bandmates: sustenance for the all-nighter they were pulling to record a few of their songs in an on-campus studio. Emily suggested we take a trip to a nearby park of giant rocks—conglomerates of limestone and red, pink, and white sandstones.

"Let's do it. Once I finish cooking this and drop it off for the band, I'll be ready."

I walked out the door in warm boots and wool socks, thick black leggings, a knee-length down coat. Emily, wearing jean shorts over gray cable-knit tights and red wool clogs without socks, put on her navy-blue peacoat.

When we arrived at the park I followed her up a rocky slope of red dust, past gnarled pines and shrunken trees still holding on to a few skeletal leaves at 6,400 feet above sea level. The rock formation ahead of us looked like the remains of a crumbled brick wall. In its center was a hole— into which Emily climbed.

"It's so windy up here!" she called down. "I want to take some pictures!"

We switched places. I sat in the rock window, puffed out my cheeks and pulled my ears to make a face like a monkey. She looked up and laughed. Then set a self-timer, ran up to sit next to me.

As we headed back to the car, Emily walked ahead of me. "Wait, I want to take one of you!" I said.

She paused, then handed over her camera and said, "Okay, go ahead." Stuck out her butt, put one hand on it, looked over her shoulder, and stuck her tongue out at me.

A month later, Emily messaged me to ask if one of my friends might be willing to participate in a project for photography

class. She'd decided to do a nude series of women with eating
disorders. I said probably not, but it couldn't hurt to ask. Then
Emily wrote, "I know you don't have an ED, but if you wanted
or would be willing to do it, too, I would love that. But I completely get if it's weird or anything."

"I mean, I do have one," I replied. "So yeah, I'll do it."

"Sorry, I wasn't meaning to minimize your issues with
eating. Just didn't know where you were with it, I guess."

Neither did I. For the photo shoot, I knocked on the door
of the small room Emily had reserved in the arts building.
The sliver of glass window was papered over. Emily opened
the door. I entered. "You only have to take off as much as
you're comfortable with," she said, casual, professional, like
a masseuse used to working with unclothed bodies. "I'll be
back in a minute."

I wanted to be brave, so I took off everything. Curled my
knees to hide my chest, wrapped my arms around my knees,
crossed my ankles. There was a white sheet, a photography
umbrella, a bright light—a setup similar to the school portraits
for which we used to tilt chins and square shoulders. She came
back in and locked the door. "Do whatever feels natural. I'm
going to start taking pictures, but you don't have to pose."

Nothing felt natural. As little kids, we had bathed together;
once, on a family trip, we stripped down together in the dark
and jumped into the Caribbean Sea. Never had she focused
in on my nipples, navel, kneecaps. I let my body straighten,
unfurled my arms, and laughed awkwardly as she tried to
calm and comfort me.

I went to see the exhibition when it went up in mid-
April. On my walk over to the arts building, one of J's bandmates yelled out "Hey, I saw you in there!" as he biked past
me. I felt nervous. How did he know it was me? What part
of my body did he see?

The prints were of women's spines, hips, bottoms, breasts, ribs. And then there was me: shoulder, collarbone, neck, chin, smile. A different mode of vulnerability.

After the show, she gave me a matted print of the photo. On the back, she wrote a note.

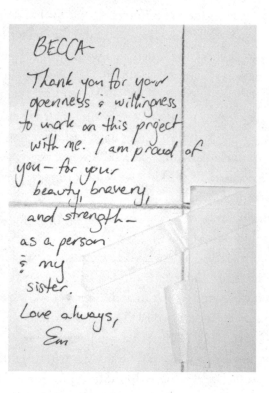

WHEN I GRADUATED IN MAY, I took a job as a special education teacher at a public high school just outside of New Orleans. The location was random. Save for a handful of acquaintances from college who'd also moved to the city, I knew no one there. But it was where the organization that was teaching me to be a teacher said I was most needed, and I was amenable. Like Colorado, Louisiana was far enough away that visits with my parents would occur very occasionally.

I had been to New Orleans only once before, when my mother, stepfather, Emily, Ches, and I joined my aunt and uncle for a Thanksgiving hosted by their friends, a middle-aged couple who lived in a large house in the Garden District with coral-colored dining room walls and an impressive collection of antique dolls. That weekend we ate beignets and wandered through the French Market, a tourist trap of alligator jerky and voodoo that led us to a shop that only sold hot sauces, all of which could be sampled by dipping damp pieces of popcorn into small pools of liquid that ranged from bold red to peppery orange to bright green.

"Look out! This one is the world's hottest sauce," said my stepfather, grinning and pointing to a bottle with a yellow-and-red label on which there was a red chili pepper lying beneath an umbrella on the beach, wearing sunglasses. It read: "Dave's Gourmet Insanity Sauce."

"I bet it's not even that hot," I scoffed. I grabbed a piece of popcorn and submerged it in the sauce. Popped it into my mouth.

Within seconds came the heat. My tears were involuntary, and my stepfather's laughter was long and loud, though not without sympathy. He offered me water, milk, bread, but nothing helped.

Nine years later, I was living in a house in the Bywater with two roommates and my own bathroom. My alarm went off at 4:15 most mornings: I'd finish prepping lessons, then drive to the empty school building in the dark, blasting a YouTube video of an Avicii and Nicky Romero song titled "Fuck School" and fantasizing that I'd crash into a tree. I wanted so badly to get in an accident in which no one was hurt but me—not bad enough to die, just bad enough to get me out of a few weeks or months of teaching.

Quitting was tempting, but not a real option—I'd never quit anything before in my life. In high school, I'd participated in every extracurricular activity available to me: field hockey, swimming, marching band, softball, track; math league, school musicals, student council, Relay For Life, Interact; all the honor societies. Throughout college, I'd worked as a peer writing center tutor and led two student organizations. I'd completed one marathon and three halves. There was no precedent for anything less than endurance.

Instead of leaving, I slogged through a thick depression, spent weeks drinking only cayenne-maple-lemon water, came home after work on Fridays, ate slice upon slice of my roommates' leftover pizza, and threw it all up. I bought bags of granola from Whole Foods and ate them alone in my car. Every few days I called my mother to solicit her advice as a school counselor. I sat outside of my house in my parked car, unable to move. I cried. I got into three car accidents. I ran another half-marathon. I adopted a dog.

In November, Emily came to visit. She'd received a grant from the college to conduct research at a nonprofit arts center, but much of the three weeks she spent in New Orleans was spent on a spare mattress in my living room. It was unclear whether she was depressed or simply exhausted. Still, she helped me take care of my ten-month-old puppy, framed art to hang on the bare walls of my bedroom, and packed me lunches, forcing me to eat.

The week of Thanksgiving, Emily flew with me and my dog from New Orleans to Philadelphia. One evening, we sat in front of the fireplace at our mother's house playing Bananagrams with Ches, who was small for thirteen, their hair white blond, eyes, behind glasses, blue like our mom's. They wore a yellow World Cup T-shirt that had been mine when I was eight. Emily wore my dark-blue sweater and her own dark-wash jeans, plus a pair of tan moccasin boots she liked to steal from me; her brown hair was cropped. The two of them sat cross-legged beside each other, working as a team. My dog came into the room and sniffed at the tiles laid out in patterns of words on the blue-and-peach-colored rug, then began to lick them. Emily said, "Don't eat Bananagrams, you toddler!" and the dog licked her cheek. I smiled. Ches cracked up.

It wasn't until February that I began to feel like I might make it through the school year. J had decided to move to the city after a noncommittal autumn, and we'd found a sweet house near City Park to rent: a half of a double shotgun painted dark green with an attic window composed of a tiny row of stained-glass squares. One Saturday morning, I went for a run in a T-shirt and shorts: Spanish moss hung gray green from the branches of massive oak trees, the scent of gardenias and crepe myrtle lingered on fences and street signs, confused white egrets nested on the neutral ground, bananas and satsumas sat in a state of languid green. A second line parade blocked traffic for miles; boys danced on rooftops in white tank tops while moms and dads and aunts and uncles sipped mixed drinks and cold drinks and smoked cigarillos below. There were trumpets, trombones, saxophones, and tubas. Drums and sirens. I was overcome with the feeling of being exactly where I wanted to be.

Emily visited again the next weekend. Along with J, we cooked breakfasts of sweet cinnamon quinoa and baked eggs and ate them on the back porch in the sun. We spent afternoons walking through City Park, sampled beers at a brewery, and wandered through the late-night art market between bars on Frenchmen Street. It was cold enough for boots, for hats, for sweaters.

Eleven months before Emily's death, it was the end of April and already unbearably hot outside. J was in the kitchen. I was lying down. The AC unit hummed and hiccuped from the window by the foot of the bed. The muscles in my lower back were spasming—it hurt so much I felt faint when I tried to walk. It wasn't clear what had brought this on, but it also wasn't the first time it had happened. Perhaps it had been a particularly bad day at work, or perhaps J and I had gotten into a fight. Regardless of the reason, I was disconsolate, stuck.

My phone rang. I saw that it was Emily, but it was late and I was exhausted. I ignored it. I assumed she was calling to check on me—the day before she'd listened patiently while I sat on my front porch sobbing into the phone. I went to bed.

Early the next morning, I got another call on my way into work. This one from my mom. "She's okay, but something happened. Emily asked me to tell you."

I cried through the rest of my drive and flew out to Colorado that weekend. Emily picked me up from the Denver airport. We ate dinner from a Whole Foods salad bar and got pedicures paid for by our mom. I slept in a sleeping bag on the tile floor of her dorm room beneath her lofted bed and popped muscle relaxants to try to get the paralyzing spasms to subside. I was trying to be there for Emily every way I knew how: I gave her a miniature bottle of rose absolute essential oil, which was labeled "fortifying," and convinced her to take the sleeping pills that she didn't like to take because they left her stuck in her nightmares. The week before she hadn't been taking them, which was why she couldn't sleep at 2 a.m., which was why she went on a walk and smoked a cigarette, which was why a man asked to bum one, which was why she stopped to offer her pack and then he threatened her with a knife and pulled her from the sidewalk and pushed her behind a bush and slipped his fingers inside of her, for which there is no reason why.

DURING THE SUMMER THAT FOLLOWED the assault, Emily returned to work at the organic farm in Maine where she'd spent the previous summer. She was still there the night before I was set to begin my second year of teaching. It was August and oppressively hot, even—especially—in the dark. I sat on my bed and opened my work-issued laptop, trying to mentally prepare.

J was in Maine, too, a few hours northeast of the farm, with his band and our dog, rehearsing for a performance at the Blackfly Ball, a costume dance party held during the annual Machias Wild Blueberry Festival. We'd been in different places for most of the summer, and for the past two weeks I'd been alone in our house. I'd never lived by myself before—I'd always had at least one roommate or pet. I loved the solitude but feared my own company. I started to look up plane ticket prices, apprehensive about the new school year, already ready to leave.

To fly to Bangor from New Orleans in five days would be almost $800—a fortune on a teacher's salary. But I was twenty-three and unencumbered. I convinced myself that the time I'd get to spend with J and Emily, the two people most important to me, was worth the cost. I told Emily my plan, both so I could see her and so she could help me make the visit a surprise for J. The night before my flight, she sent me a text: "I'm really really sorry but I screwed up and accidentally said something to J." I got mad and then I got over it by midnight on Friday, when I arrived in Maine.

Emily was there waiting for me at the airport. We squeezed hard and tight, got into the small silver car that Emily had paid extra to rent as a driver under twenty-five. We were headed to J's parents' house, where he and the band were staying, about an hour away. At some point we found ourselves on a dead-end rural road without cell service. I saw nothing that I recognized. Lost but adrenalized, we blasted ridiculous music like Britney Spears's "Toxic." Then a song I didn't know came on and Emily said, "Okay—you can't not dance to this one." She turned up the volume. Guitar and harmonica, then kick drum, tambourine—when the snare and cymbals joined for the chorus we bounced beneath our seat belts like kids on a trampoline.

We arrived at 1:33 a.m. J opened the door and our dog bounded down the long staircase. I crouched down to greet her in my floral skirt and high-heeled cowboy boots, and she bowled me over; licked my face so thoroughly I could barely breathe.

J laughed and said, "How am I supposed to make any kind of impression after this?" Then, noticing Emily behind me, the dog welcomed her with equally sloppy enthusiasm.

"That's up my nose! That's my nose!" Emily laughed.

At the festival on Saturday night, we danced and drank, sang and stayed up way too late. J and I slept in a tent. Emily slept in the rental car. I felt guilty leaving her alone—I thought she would be cold and cramped. She swore she was okay. And anyway, she said, since we had to leave early the next morning, it was probably the best way to ensure she'd be awake on time.

As she drove me to the airport, Emily told me that she had been accused of stealing from her coworkers at the farm: sunglasses, a passport, a jacket. She had borrowed the sunglasses without asking, but she'd meant to—to ask. She forgot to return them, admitted she messed up, and gave them back. And, yes, she did have a history of theft, but it had all been related to her eating disorder, wrapped up in restriction, numbness, control. "I'm an easy target," she said. She knew nothing about the other missing items. Even so, her boss "kept implying I didn't really feel bad and that it was all an act and stuff. I think that was the worst part."

But she was already excited to apply to be an apprentice at a different organic farm next summer, one that grew heirloom tomatoes and fairy tale eggplants.

We laughed, then, about how the situation was so similar to what we'd grown up with: how if something went missing, maybe a necklace, pen, or pair of socks, our mother accused us of theft and assumed we were more likely lying to her than truly innocent. (Occasionally, one of us had taken the object in question; far more often, we had not.) We talked about the approaching academic year—about leaving the farm, where Emily felt balanced, safe, and healthy, and returning to the campus where she'd been busy and stressed and assaulted in the spring. She was nervous about how she would handle the transition, what it would be like to be back there for a third year.

We hugged goodbye, said, "Love, love, love." We didn't know what was coming. We couldn't have known what we didn't know.

After we parted ways in Maine, Emily made her way to Delaware to spend the last few days of her summer break at home with our family. It was just past ten o'clock at night in New Orleans when she called. I knew right away something was up.

"What's wrong?"

"Mom blamed me for the assault."

"What? What do you mean?"

"She basically told me it was my fault. That I was 'artfully lying' and if I hadn't been walking around outside late at night it wouldn't have happened."

"Jesus Christ," I began to rant. "I can't believe she'd say that. I mean, you know that's not true—we both know that's not true. It's not your fault. It doesn't matter what you did or didn't do." I was on edge. "I'm going to call Mom."

Emily said she wasn't so sure that was a good idea, but I didn't care. The call went straight to voicemail. After the tone, I started to speak: "How dare you—how could you ever say that it's Emily's fault—that's so fucked up, Mom."

I hung up, took a deep breath, and realized this would not end well for either of us.

Our mother could be vindictive, kept her moods as currency. She held us responsible for her feelings—anything we said or did that she took personally. Still, growing up, our mother always got to be good—in comparison, our father was the bad guy. But good came with consequence: thick, defensive walls and strict rules. No dessert unless we ate our vegetables, cleared our plates. The completion of extra chores as restitution for the time we caused her to waste. She accused me and Emily of being manipulative, of lying to her. A bit of a low-grade persecution complex. I learned to feel guilty, learned to doubt my own motives. We watched her find fault with her thighs in dressing rooms and learned to dislike our bodies. We heard her doubt the sincerity of compliments and learned to believe that anything nice someone said to us couldn't possibly be meant.

I texted Emily: "I hope I didn't make it worse for you by leaving that message. I'm sorry. I wasn't thinking clearly. I'm afraid of what they'll do to you because of that."

She wrote back: "No it's OK, I don't really care. She should hear how upset you are so she knows it's not just me. Or she'll literally think I misconstrued the whole thing which is why you were so upset. In which case, let her think that, I don't care."

Years after Emily died, we talked about this incident, my mother and I. It came up in one of the many conversations I had with my family once I started to write this book. I was constantly seeking triggers for my memory, paths to places I didn't know I'd forgotten—anything that might help set the story straight. I sifted through everything: photo albums both concrete and digital, messages and posts on social media, letters and cards either written or received by members of my family, old journal entries, receipts, flight itineraries, emails, chat transcripts, and texts. I asked people who knew Emily to share with me their own interpretations of the past, their own memories.

It's possible I'm mistaken, but had I not been writing about my grief, our loss, I don't believe I would have had an occasion to ask questions, and without an occasion, I wouldn't have asked. Too risky. It's not sufficient, the wanting, to overcome the lonely wondering, the fear of what will be unearthed, the missing, the hurt.

My mother was the one who brought up the voicemail I'd left her. She told me she knew Emily had tried to keep her from it; she found it in her deleted messages. She wanted to know what Emily had told me about their conversation. When I recounted what I remembered, she said, "You never asked for my version." Claimed she'd never said the assault was Emily's fault, that she was just trying to express her concern about Emily's ability to maintain her health when she returned to campus. Thought Emily, already prone to misinterpreting words and deeds as slights, latched on to the one thing she said about taking a walk at 2 a.m. and missed the rest. Thought Emily was in the early stages of her one and only full-blown manic episode, thought it must have started out slow. She theorized that Emily had stopped taking her medications over the summer while working at the farm in Maine.

And though there is no proof, and though it hadn't occurred to me (I tended to trust my sister's ability to care for herself more than our mother did), I can imagine, easily, the core of Emily—impulsive, all-or-nothing, quick to react—feeling consistently good and deciding she could take herself off her meds. Earlier that August, she'd written:

> Sitting by the fire, listening to Typhoon, drinking IPAs, and laughing with friends about giant yellow spiders and *Waiting for Guffman*, I became overwhelmingly grateful for my life. I am in that mindset where I am EXACTLY where I want to be. My body feels great—besides the soreness of my back and neck, but I guess that's a given with farming. I am scared to go back to school, scared I'll lose this, but I want to be grateful in those hard moments that I've had this, can have this, and *will* have this again. I am strong; I am capable; I am capable of this growth. This perpetual stretching.

In other words, it's quite possible our mother is right, but to set it in type makes me uneasy. I feel like I'm betraying Emily.

By MID-SEPTEMBER, EMILY TOLD ME she was swimming every day, eating a lot, and still losing weight. On the phone, she said, "I wonder if this is what it's like to be manic. I mean, I feel great but, like, normal and not out of control, so I don't think I am, but I sort of get it." She was hosting dinner parties for friends every night, buying dozens of books (among them: *Modeling Life*, *The Beekeeper's Bible*, and two copies of the *Next to Normal* Broadway musical script) and ordering live plants from the internet: English lavender, bee balm, lemon balm, lemongrass, lemon thyme, a Meyer lemon tree, apple mint. She started sharing photos on Instagram at 3 a.m. of kitchen counters filled with produce—watermelon, acorn squash, potatoes, kale, apples, zucchini, and tomatoes (which she never even liked). She shaved her head and claimed, "It helps my thoughts come in more clearly." She wasn't taking her meds because she said her doctors said she didn't need them; she was the best she'd ever been in her life. She told me, "People are afraid of what is good because it makes them self-examine, and I can't carry that right now. I feel like I'm being watched all the time," which was both nonsensical and paranoid.

She sent an indecipherable letter to J. She sent an email to the president of the college with a plan for how to fix everything for everyone. Because she was 25 percent coherent, she was turned away from a psychiatric hospital.

After I got home from work on a Friday afternoon, I called one of Emily's roommates. "I'm sorry to bother you like this, but nothing that Emily is telling me makes any sense and I'm worried. Do you have any idea what's going on?"

"There are rotten apple cores all over the countertops," the roommate said, "and I don't think she's sleeping. Our RA keeps knocking on the door, so she won't stay here anymore. I'm not sure where she goes, but she hasn't cleaned her cat's litter box in weeks and, honestly, I'm scared for her. She thinks she's totally fine and won't let anyone help her."

The roommate said she didn't know what to do—and neither did I. The fear was invasive, consuming—it crawled through my core to the tips of my fingers, gnawed at my nails until there was nothing left but legs and ears. So I put in headphones with the volume turned all the way up and ran past puddles. Fallen oak branches, missing railroad ties, shrieking geese. The air by the lake carried the scent of fried dough and powdered sugar. I ended up back on my front porch. Stared past blocks of ivy as sweat slid down my cheeks. I wanted to cry.

The front door opened, and J joined me. "Hey."

I said nothing.

"Are you okay?"

I told him I was thinking about Emily. How she couldn't slow herself down. He said maybe it wasn't such a terrible thing to have so much energy. To be so high.

"You don't understand," I said. "She's like a train that's too fast for its tracks."

"Well . . . are you all right?" he asked.

"Yeah. Fine. Just tired." I shrugged and pressed my lips into a smile.

On Saturday night, J and I attended my friend's twenty-third birthday party. We got there late enough that everyone was already drunk and high, especially the birthday boy. Most of the people there were teachers primed for weekend revelry. The kitchen counters were covered: red Solo cups, lukewarm cans of beer, half-empty handles, lidless tubs of melting ice cream, blue-frosted cupcakes abandoned after one bite.

For a while I stood and listened to acquaintances recount stories about their students, then I helped myself to dessert. Once I started, I kept going, but no one was paying attention. I headed down the hallway to the bathroom, locked the door. Stared in the mirror and asked "What are you doing?" and answered myself over the toilet, headfirst.

This was not how I wanted to be, but the illusion of control, its loss and recovery, is addictive. My first taste of it came in college. Each year, the dean of students hosted a holiday dinner for the members of the student government. His home was warm and clean and full of lighted candles on the edge of a dark winter campus. Silver trays of rich foods: carved birds and braised brisket, roasted sweet potatoes and buttered green beans, hearty loaves of bread and light angel food cakes, latticed pies and dark chocolate brownies. And more and more and on and on and everywhere. On the walls, autographed photographs of people important or famous.

During my sophomore year, I went home from one of these dinners filled with sautéed greens and macaroni and a deep, heavy discomfort. I remember the walk back as cold and quiet, the campus as softened by snow. I don't know how I made the decision to stick my fingers down my throat. It seemed like it would provide relief; a short-term solution, nothing more. But I continued to do it—first for months, then for years. How did no one know what I was doing? The sound is urgent, like an exorcism, like someone drowning, gasping for breath. It is explosion and release. Then again, such upheaval is almost expected in college: hangovers in the morning after too much to drink at night, communal spaces filled with the sweet and sour smell of regurgitated red punch. Then again, I might have liked the secret.

When I came out of the bathroom, I found J on the outskirts of a conversation beside the kitchen table. He didn't know anyone at the party well. When I whispered "I'm ready to leave" into his dark curls, he caught the sharp mint of mouthwash on my breath.

"What were you doing in there?" he said, nodding toward the hallway.

"Nothing." I shrugged.

"You all right?"

"Yeah, fine. Just tired."

J finished the can of beer he was holding, put it down, and held my hand. We walked away from the party in silence. There was nothing to say. By which I mean that everything I wanted to say was meant for Emily: Get your shit together. Stop being crazy—stop being sick all the time. Get better before you get worse. Or at least get worse so you can get treatment.

At 5:47 p.m. the next day, an email from Emily arrived in my inbox. The subject line: road trip plans! Inside was just the line "More info to come. Love you all." And at the bottom an attachment titled "Emily's Apartment/Life Timeline." The document was a confusing list composed of outlandish claims (like "I am financially and medically stable; checking in with my therapist for an appointment on Tuesday/doctor/family before I leave" and "Potentially graduating this semester or year, but no decisions until returned from road trip") and tasks she intended to complete over the next four days ("Get tested with Planned Parenthood"; "Fix car"; "Figure out who I'm staying with in CO, on east coast").

What to do with this was beyond me. I forwarded the message to my mother and stepfather. On Monday evening, my mother called.

"Did you see what I sent?" I asked.

"Yes—she sent us the same thing," my mother said. She sounded tired, worried.

"Okay, but what the fuck even is this? Can her car make it out of the state? Where's she going to stay?"

"I hear you. The goal right now is to get her to at least stay in Colorado so her therapist can keep an eye on her. We've told her she can't miss an appointment."

"Like that'll do anything."

I paced around my kitchen, reaching up to open the doors of cabinets and closing them again, opening the door of the refrigerator and peering into bright lights and glass and plastic. Nothing ever changed. It was something to do with the feeling, an energy squirrelly and angry, laced with frustration and fear.

"Well I don't have a lot of options, Becca. She's completely shut us out. She hasn't picked up my calls or responded to any of my messages."

"Yeah, I know. I've experienced it."

"Please talk to her. We need to try to convince her to stay in Colorado. See if you can get through to her."

"Oh so you think she'll listen to me? I'm lucky if I get a response to a text these days. Even when I hear from her, it's impossible to have a conversation. She's all over the place."

My mother sighed. "Just try, okay?"

At work on Tuesday morning, I disappeared to the empty teacher's lounge. The photocopier clicked and shuffled papers into piles; I sat down at a round table in a blue plastic chair, beneath pocked white ceiling tiles and skinny tubes of fluorescence. I pulled from my bag my laptop and an orange. Set the computer down on the table, slid the edge of my right thumbnail into the fruit, felt the give of tough skin, the release of mist. When I opened my Gmail account, I saw that Emily was online. I said hi. Several minutes later, she responded.

hi sorry

trying to look at houses and freaking out about art and
getting sick and my apartment mates are being ridiculous

wait what

i thought you loved your apartment?

i'm sorry you're getting sick

i do but theyre stupid about money and throwing away
my shit and micromanaging me

and i love them dearly but i need to live by myself

and off campus in general

and i feel aaaaawful sick

but have so much fucking art to do and i cant miss class
either

idk. im fine im just struggling.

if you're getting sick, have you thought about just
laying low and recovering for a couple days?

im gonna but i need to find a place and move out

i really do love them but i cant live with them

and more than anything, admin wont leave them alone
which just isnt fair because it's about me

they get called and my rlc keeps stopping by and idk. its
just a mess

em

i know you don't want to hear this

but i'm concerned about you too

well that's fine but i'm fine

classes are just stressful right now and no one will leave
me alone.

yeah but this hasn't just been the past couple of days,
it's been weeks

no

ive been fine except for administration.

actually.

and truthfully i love you but dont want to explain this
for the millionth time. i'm fine. i'm actually really great,
i just need space from this school

okay. i'm just telling you i'm concerned

and that i think that staying near people like your
therapist who can be supportive is a good way to show
that you really are fine

that's fine. but i'm telling you i'm far more of an introvert
than people understand and this attention is driving me
fucking insane.

i know that. and i have an appointment with her today
and have texted her all weekend

I believe you. i honestly do

and i think that it would drive me nuts too

but leaving just makes people even more concerned

just saying. i'm on your side. I promise

it just sucks. im getting blamed for things i havent done,
i get watched and called and texted ALL the time by
EVERYONE. it sucks. i need to leave because i need
room to breathe

im really ok and im being so safe and responsible and
careful about this trip. but i've always wanted to do it and
i need to be really actually alone

that's fine

i'm still telling you, as someone who loves you more than
anyone else in the world and thinks you're incredible, that
i'm concerned about you. i just need you to know that

i know that

and i understand

right now literally the only things wrong are me needing
space, feeling really sick (even though i'm sleeping/
eating/exercising plenty), and art that's become hard

i dont want to isolate myself, i'll still be in touch and be
over at this apartment a lot, but i really really need space.
badly

it feels shitty to be somewhere that doesnt want you

like i cant even describe how quickly and positively this
school has changed, for soooo many reasons

why do you think they don't want you?

and people are scared of that, and i'm a very, very easy
scapegoat

they told me i needed to be in a hospital or leave. which
i'm not willing to do at all

and my doctors dont think i need it

what have your doctors said, exactly?

that i'm basically overmedicated, which i am

because my body is already producing all the chemicals it needs

i was supposed to go off meds in three months

but i'm weaning off now instead

and i've known that and kept saying that but everyone (ie the school) just thinks im manic.

which im really truly not

and the bottom line which no one seems to understand or want to accept is that i know myself better than anyone because ive spent a long time figuring that out

it doesnt mean i cant misjudge myself or have clouded thinking

but i know im ok

yeah

but a couple weeks ago you also told me you were worried you might be manic

do you remember?

and now, if everyone is saying that, is there a possibility you might've been right?

i remember. but ive realized i just get excited. really
easily. but i also know when i want to experience my
emotions and when i need to compartmentalize

i just see a lot of connections in everything. all the time.
it's really overwhelming and despite a lot of amazing
support, REALLY fucking lonely

i believe it

like i genuinely feel like a freak show sometimes. people
don't follow my thinking and i hate it. and i work really
hard to communicate in a way that makes sense but
people just dont get it

i just miss feeling normal and underwhelmed

yeah, i've felt that way before, too

what do you mean normal and underwhelmed?

like nobody SEES anything or listens or pays attention.
at least not as often as i do. i literally see everything
as shapes and colors and lines now. and i think i have
photographic memory and it's just a lot all at once so i
need to take time alone to process it

idk. i just have never been this stimulated

i just am wondering why all of a sudden this has
changed, you know?

meds, mania, whatever it is

i really believe im just healthier than ive ever been

my brain and body and everything are just finally clicking

and it's always been there, you know i've always been
"intense" or whatever

but im eating and sleeping and spending time with
people and just want to soak everything in more than i
ever have

yeah, and that's good

it's just a little overwhelming

for you too, it seems

yeah, it is

but it wasn't unmanageable at ALL until the school got
involved

and i find it ironic that they didnt give a shit when i
was super depressed for two years but now that im
challenging things and so are other people, it's an issue

change is scary because it means they have to be open
to it, and administration isnt ready

and setting an ultimatum without fair warning is a load
of shit

what ultimatum?

that i need to be in the hospital or leave

so i told them i'd leave because a hospital would be
HORRIBLE for me right now

and if my doctors are saying otherwise, shouldnt that matter?

what is this change that you keep talking about? that is so scary, apparently, for everyone

i dont really know how to describe it except that students are really supporting and trusting each other and being really really honest and any forum for discussion is soooo engaged and interesting, people are going to talks more than i've ever seen at least, student government office hours are ALWAYS full

everyone has become increasingly more supportive, honest, VOCAL, and involved

which means administration is being challenged in a number of ways. and they aren't ready

i don't understand why you need to leave if you're a part of something that you think is really good

because they told me i needed to or i needed to be in the hospital

im coming back, im staying in touch

but i cant be here now because im not welcome

it doesn't sound to me like you're not welcome... it just sounds like they are worried about you

listen, i need to go soon. is there anything else you want me to know or understand?

i'm listening

it's fine. i gotta go too

we can talk later

i just feel shitty

i'm here for you

and i'm concerned about you

but i know you will be okay, whatever happens

well thanks i guess.

you do need to know im not hurting or going to hurt
myself or anyone else

and im more honest than i've ever been in my entire life.

so i will be ok.

okay. i love you

love you too. thanks for listening.

I stood up from my chair, left the room, turned right, then left, then walked down a long hallway. Locked the door to the faculty restroom and turned on the light. The mirror showed me waxen. My shoulders began to fold. My stomach burned, tense with orange acid. Doubt and fear: *What if I'm just like everyone else who will not listen?* What if she was really seeing more clearly than the school administration—afraid of change, invested in the status quo of structures, in keeping power locked in empty closets and sending into exile anyone who thought she'd found the key. What if I could only see what was on the surface? What if Emily had already climbed down the ladder, was breathing her own air, body black with ocean, exploring lines and shapes and colors, not holding to a course.

MY SISTER AND I SAT ALONE in our father's Prius, parked outside of a Starbucks with the heat turned up. It was the day before Thanksgiving. We took the lids off our cups to let the liquid cool and held them below our noses, breathing in the smell of coffee.

"So how are you feeling?" I asked.

She began to detail the fallout from her two-month-long manic episode: her feeling that she'd alienated all of her friends on campus, her fears about not finding someone to live with next year, and the impending "talk" with our mother and stepfather about the money she owed them for car insurance and prescriptions and therapy appointments and a meal plan. And also the classes she hadn't completed, how she'd have to pay for them.

She paused to twist her mouth to one side, then said, "I know I messed up, but it doesn't make any sense to turn my illness into a lesson about responsibility."

I shook my head in agreement. This approach to care felt nowhere close to fair. "It's going to be shitty, but you will get through it," I reminded her. "It's going to be okay in the end."

She shrugged and looked down at her dirty chai latte. "I guess." Lifted it to her lips, took a sip. Then opened her mouth, letting the liquid fall from her tongue back into the cup. "Ouch! Too hot!"

I started to laugh and so did she. It was nice to be able to have a real conversation with Emily—it felt like my sister had come back to herself, back to me.

The next day, Emily and I made the pilgrimage together in the back seat of our father and stepmother's car, as we'd done many times before, to Thanksgiving at our aunt and uncle's. Their house, which used to be a barn, is made of wood and glass with suspect steps that lead to an indoor balcony, a place to stand and be observed from twenty feet below. As kids, Emily, our cousins, and I used to perform from this makeshift stage: we'd sing songs or do magic tricks straight from a kit or act out improvised skits that we never finished because we made ourselves laugh too hard.

How oddly large her ears always appeared to me during that three-hour car ride, like they belonged to an old person; she'd sleep open-mouthed, her head tucked into the door. We'd find ways to lean on each other so we could get something close to comfortable and did our best to ignore our father's road rage and the stomach-tossing way he sped on roads that wound through fields of horses and mushroom farms.

When we arrived, we ate pigs in a Pillsbury blanket and stuffed mushrooms made by our grandmother, crackers and locally crafted cheeses and dried apricots and duck sausage, aluminum tubs of brussels sprouts and barley and brisket and turkey and mashed potatoes and stuffing, boats of gravy, a tub of Magnolia Bakery's banana pudding, and a dozen sweet, buttery pie crusts. After the meal, we curled up with our cousins on a leather couch and giggled. That night, Emily's happiness was believable. I believed it.

Four days after Thanksgiving, Emily was back in Colorado and I was back in New Orleans with J, at a red beans and rice dinner that our friends hosted each week. My phone vibrated in the back right pocket of my jeans. It was my sister. I stepped outside into the cold and dark to take the call, white plastic spoon and Styrofoam bowl of warm, vinegary mush in hand, and sat on the back steps.

"Hey, Em. How are you?" I asked.

"I'm okay. How are you?"

"I'm okay too. What's up?"

"Nothing. Just feeling low in general. What about you?"

"Kinda the same. But I'm, like, fine. So I don't know what's wrong with me. You know?" I said. I took a bite of beans.

"Yeah, I do."

"I want to feel better!"

"Me too. The sad part is being manic felt so much better. It was crazy, I know, but at least I felt good and wanted to be doing the things I'm doing. Now I just feel like everything is deeply overwhelming and I have no energy."

"I know manic felt good, but it was scary. And I also know you can handle anything. Even what feels overwhelming. I know because I've seen you do it."

"Yeah. I think I can, I just don't want to. I don't even really want to be here at school at all, either, which feels shitty," Emily said.

"Yeah, I get that. Why don't you want to be there?"

"I don't know—it just feels overwhelming and endless and not like something that means anything to me. But I'm afraid to take time off because I know I won't want to come back. It seems like nothing is going well. It's hard to keep going."

"But you love your art classes, don't you?"

"I do, but I'm really, really unmotivated. And, I don't know . . . If I actually knew where I was living next year or felt like I wanted to be taking classes or like there were people who wanted to spend time with me, or if I felt financially stable or had any money at all—if I weren't depressed for what seems like no reason . . ."

"Then what?"

"I don't know. I don't know. I just want to graduate. I just want to get this all over with. Like apparently I can't find a happy middle here, you know?"

"One day at a time. Honestly, I don't think it's necessarily the place. Remember what you told me? That if you can figure out how to be okay where you are, then you're set?" I said.

"I know you're right. I just feel like I can't get out of this," said Emily.

"That may be true, but you still have choices, even when there's something you're stuck with. And you can do it."

"Poop. Well, thanks. I think I'm going to head to bed. I love you though—thanks for listening."

"Anytime. I love you always. Get some sleep. And, hey— just one more thing. It's okay to feel shitty. But don't give up on yourself, or yourself at school. It gets better, and it all feels worth it in the end."

"I hope so. And I trust you, so that's something."

After we hung up, I stayed in my seat on the steps, wiping away reflexive tears. One of the dinner's hosts popped his head out the door and asked if everything was all right. I explained that I was okay, just worried about my sister, who had a long history of mental illness. He said something kind and kind of comforting: "Hey, that's okay, I can relate. My brother went through [this] and [this] and [this]. And now he has his shit together, but, yeah . . . It sucks, man."

FOR CHRISTMAS, OUR AUNT, UNCLE, COUSINS, and grandparents came to our father and stepmother's house, all excess and festivity: star-topped tree draped in tinsel, presents piled high, Christmas songs beneath the rip of wrapping paper, a spread of takeout from the Peking duck restaurant in Philadelphia's Chinatown that both of my parents had been patronizing since college (first together, then separately)— platters full of fried spring rolls, sweet and sticky barbecue spare ribs, taut string beans in piquant garlic sauce, house fried rice, and the salty broth of wonton soup. Once we'd eaten and all the gifts had been opened and the performance of excitement was complete, my sister, our three cousins, and J and I followed my father and his brother down to the basement to get high.

Emily had been given a wearable device designed to correct posture—her slumped shoulders a feature on which our father was forever commenting. Someone brought the gift downstairs to play with, and after each of us inhaled a cloud of marijuana vapor, it was taken out of its packaging. We teased Emily into putting it on. She smiled a little sadly and rolled her eyes. It vibrated as soon as she slouched.

Shortly after we all came up from the basement, Emily began to feel ill. She said she'd probably just gotten too high and was going to lie down and take a nap. She went upstairs to the bedroom we used to share. The rest of us played Cards Against Humanity by a fire fed with wrapping paper and needles shed from the tree. We were as amused by the game's absurdity as we were by how it scandalized our grandmother, Nana, when we finally succeeded in convincing her to play a round. She returned to her seat beside our grandfather, who fielded her disapprobation with a smile and a shrug.

The sun began to sink behind the houseplants ensconced in the seat of the living room's bay window. It occurred to me that it had been hours since we'd seen Emily. I went upstairs to check on her, knocked softly, heard no answer. Emily was unstirring beneath the comforter, nearly unconscious. I sat on the bed beside her, checked for breath, rubbed her back, and looked around the room, which had once been so familiar to me. Walls painted a bright shade of purple that our father had picked out, built-in shelves full of books he'd read aloud to us (ones like *The Hobbit, Favorite Folktales from Around the World,* and *The Collected Tales of Edgar Allan Poe*), and an overabundance of tchotchkes, from beaded Huichol masks that smelled of sweet beeswax to a wooden piggy bank shaped like a cow but painted like a frog.

As kids, we'd lie prone on the rug, propped up on our elbows, reading or drawing or playing with kids' meal toys while Emily's pet rabbit, Buster, nibbled the edges of our books or hopped over our legs. He roamed the room freely, ornamenting the corners and the space beneath our bunk bed with tiny pellets of poop. When the rabbit died, Emily was devastated. She authored and illustrated a booklet titled *Buster's Sad Life* and conducted a funeral. Our father and stepmother helped her bury him in the backyard.

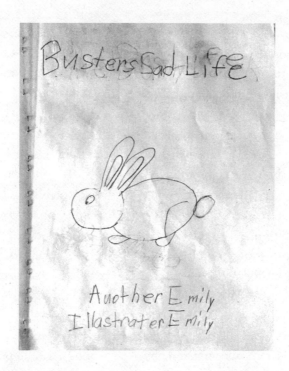

Busters Sad Life

Author Emily
Illustrater Emily

Should I have been more concerned? She'd been depressed for the better part of December—had felt herself a burden. Our mother, stepfather, and Ches were out of the country, so she was splitting her winter break between Bubbie's apartment in Philly and our father and stepmother's house. I was nervous about her staying there without me. They'd take care of her, of course—would sweetly cater to her every need. But if I wasn't there, there would be no buffer between her and our father's unpredictable temper. (Perhaps our stepmother, but I'd only ever seen her stay silent or out of the way.) I asked Emily to spend time with me and J at his parents' house, but she'd refused to come for more than an afternoon. She cited a blankness, a fear of having to make conversation out of the nothing she felt she had to say.

By the time we were both back "home" in January—Emily in Colorado, me in New Orleans—her health had declined dramatically. I was sitting on the red velvet couch in my living room when Emily texted me and said, "I don't think I want to live anymore." We weren't even a full week into the new year.

I responded immediately, listened via text and consoled and tried to convince her to hang on—tried to leverage how much she trusted me to help her believe that she was going to get through this and it was going to be worth it. I sat, worried and scared, and began to cry. And then I had to leave. J and I had plans with friends. We were running late.

J drove us through the dark to The Blind Pelican, where we sat on the vinyl seats in a wood-paneled room decorated with a miscellany of Saints gear, neon beer signs, and the mounted head of a deer. We drank brown bottles of Abita Amber Lager and ate twenty-five-cent oysters with four friends from college; that night, the six of us began to plan our Mardi Gras costumes and laughed at the photos on our old student IDs, which we all still carried in our wallets in pursuit of discounts at movie theaters and museums. When we left the restaurant, we encountered a crowd that had gathered in the cold to celebrate the beginning of carnival season. As a St. Charles streetcar full of merrymakers in costumes and masks passed, the crowd cheered and caught beads tossed through the streetcar's open windows with their outstretched gloves.

I kept Emily company the next two nights via FaceTime. I sat on the bare floor of my living room while she lay on her bed atop a multicolored, striped duvet cover that had once belonged to me. She, depressed, and I, helpless, both hardly saying anything. A ginger tabby moved into and out of the picture, alternating between kneading Emily's lap or walking across it; she had adopted him on a whim in the fall and named him Curry. She was able to keep him because she'd identified a loophole that forced the school to let him live in her dorm room—a typical Emily thing.

By Thursday afternoon, Emily's passive suicidal ideation had become active. She recognized the danger, called 911, and was transported by ambulance to a behavioral hospital, where she was monitored for a week, after which her health insurance would no longer pay for the stay. Upon her release, nothing had changed. Emily kept saying she felt stuck— unable to make decisions, unsure of what to do.

My mother and I had scarcely been speaking, but we both wanted Emily alive. She sent me an email containing a clear, caring message that I was to use. She hoped that if it came from both of us, we might get through: First, our concern. Then, the recommendation to stay with our aunt and uncle in the suburbs of Denver; there, Emily wouldn't have to do anything she didn't want to do. She would be in a good, safe place until she felt better and/or not quite so stuck. Finally, the reminder that we loved her, were there for her, and would help in any way she wanted.

It worked: Emily stayed for almost a month with our stepfather's brother, a kind and caring person, and his wife, a doctor well-versed in mental illness. My uncle and oldest cousin's severe allergies, though, meant that Curry couldn't come with Emily.

When I asked my aunt how I could help, she said I could find a place for the cat to stay. This, too, was typical: my sister's impulse had become my responsibility. To send a message to someone out of the blue with an ask felt like jumping into a lake from a cliff, fully aware that the water below was ice cold. I began by reaching out to the friends of Emily's I knew best. I explained that within the past three months Emily had had both a serious manic episode—which I assumed they all

knew—and now a serious depressive episode, which may have
been news to them. She was waiting it out at our aunt and
uncle's house until her new meds kicked in and balanced
her brain chemistry. We didn't know exactly how long it was
going to take—could any of them take care of Curry for a
while? Did they know someone who might be able to?

It took two days to find a temporary home for the cat.
Meanwhile, Emily all but entirely stopped responding to my
messages and calls. The one time she did answer me over
the course of the next three weeks, she said she was bored
but didn't have the energy to do anything except sit around
on a couch with our aunt and watch mindless TV or go out
with our grandparents, who lived nearby, when they managed to drag her to a meal or a movie.

By the middle of February, Emily was itching to go back
to school. But she was also nervous about her ability to handle
the pressures and responsibilities of class and the writing center
and student government and GROW. On February 13, I forwarded to her an email containing a quote that I thought she
might find encouraging: "Decide that you want it more than
you are afraid of it." Three days later, she returned to campus.

Had I known then what I know now, I would not have
sent this quote. For one thing, it is attributed to Bill Cosby;
for another, the "it" is unspecified.

THE THIRD TIME EMILY CAME to NEW ORLEANS was during her spring break. But she wasn't there, really: she arrived blank, a body only, on a Thursday afternoon in the middle of March while I was still at work. She waited for an hour as I made my way from the high school to the airport through rush hour traffic. I was so flustered by my own lateness that when she opened the passenger door of my small white car, instead of saying hi, I said sorry. She reassured me she didn't mind.

In the evening we wandered in the sun by Bayou Saint John, through Mid-City neighborhoods. In front of a huge house with bright turquoise doors framed in orange, there was a small kumquat tree. "Have you ever tried one of these?" I asked, twisting a single fruit gently from a slender branch.

She shook her head.

"You have to! They're so good and tart."

To humor me, she took a bite and nodded in unenthused agreement. We kept walking: down Esplanade Avenue, through a triangle-shaped green space with a wind chime and tall red sculpture, past Canseco's Market and a little Mediterranean restaurant with two outdoor tables, a wine bar that sold fancy cheeses, the salon where I got my hair cut, a coffee shop. We continued straight until we were walking along the perimeter of the Fair Grounds: black metal fencing and tall bushes, behind which hid an endless parking lot.

"Okay, now you decide: Where do you want to go?"

Emily froze.

"Do you want to turn left or continue straight ahead?"

She stared at me like an action figure who's just discovered she doesn't come with batteries. I, too, felt unsure of how to proceed.

"You must be tired . . . Why don't we just go back home?"

She agreed. Not agreed, exactly—just didn't seem to care.

On Friday, I woke up before Emily and went to work. When I returned in the afternoon, we watched several episodes from the first season of *House of Cards* and played a couple rounds of Bananagrams. I attempted to make almond milk from nuts that had been soaked in water, blended, and strained through a fine-mesh cloth and made Emily do a taste test. She took a sip, gave herself a white, watery mustache, and half laughed.

On Saturday, Emily let me bring her to the Irish Channel Parade. Together we caught green beads and bars of Irish Spring soap and whole cabbages tossed from floats that passed down Magazine Street. She held a cabbage while I got tipsy and planted kisses on the cheeks of old men in exchange for small trophies: green garters, tissue paper roses.

As we pushed our way through the crowd, I spotted someone I knew playing a game of flip cup in the front yard of a house along the parade route. I called his name and ran over to give him a hug. He said, "Come play with us!" I waited outside the gate for Emily to catch up, then grabbed her hand. I wanted to pull her into an orbit of merriment. I wanted to forget feeling responsible. She didn't want to drink. She stood beside me at the folding table and played with water in her cup instead of beer.

When the parade ended, Emily and I wandered back down the route toward my car. We bumped into KC, my friend and coworker, and her boyfriend. I asked KC to take a photo of me and my sister. I didn't know it would be the last one.

On Sunday morning, I stepped outside to call our mom while Emily was still sleeping, but she didn't pick up. I left a message in which I vented my frustration: Why had I bought a plane ticket for Emily just so she could come here and be a lump of a human? I went back inside, wrote in my journal, heard Emily sneeze from my bed, and winced: the longer she slept, the less energy I'd have to spend fueling our one-way conversations, trying to pull from her some semblance of herself, some interest in absolutely anything.

In the afternoon, we rode bikes to Lake Pontchartrain. Emily lagged behind me either because she was tired or because I wouldn't slow to her pace. On the way back, we met up with my friend JK at an abandoned disc golf course in City Park, where film production trailers sometimes set up shop. We followed JK's two dogs as they ran through the tall grass, occasionally pausing to admire the graffiti on the small concrete structures that had remained intact.

The three of us went back to my house for lunch. I started to pull things out of my fridge and told them where to find the bread, listing the ingredients I had for sandwiches: spinach, hummus, tomatoes, mustard, carrots, pickles, peanut butter, jelly.

"Has she always been like this?" JK asked Emily.

"Always. She's always been bossy," Emily said.

"But that's what we love about her. Or at least we love her anyway," said JK.

We sat in white plastic Ikea chairs around the kitchen table and ate. We sat on the couch in the living room and watched the film *Blue Jasmine*. We witnessed the slow but persistent unhinging of Jasmine; we witnessed Jasmine's husband, Hal, hang himself. The movie ended. I sat still and wondered if it was okay that we'd watched this, whether Emily was okay. It had only been two months since her hospital stay. I didn't know what she was thinking. I didn't ask.

When he'd learned Emily would be visiting me, our father invited himself to New Orleans. I was afraid to tell him not to come, so I didn't—just said that Emily already had the couch, so there wasn't room for him to stay with me. He arrived on Monday evening, picked up a rental car, and went straight to his hotel. On Tuesday, while I was at work, he took Emily to Jean Lafitte National Historical Park and Preserve to walk through a swamp full of alligator eyes. On Wednesday, their outing was to Rouses Market to buy groceries for me. That night, we went to a Pelicans game. Our seats were behind one of the baskets; we waved white thundersticks and cheered for the home team. We left the arena silly, cheerful, high on collective energy. Our father dropped us off back at my house, gave us big hugs, and said goodbye—his flight was in the morning.

Emily and I changed into pajamas, brushed our teeth. Mouth full of toothpaste, I asked, "So, how was it? How was your day?"

"Fine," she said, getting into my bed. "Dad threw a fit in the grocery store and snapped at me, of course, which was stupid."

"Seriously? What happened?"

"He got mad about a can of beans."

I spat out the toothpaste and looked at her: under the covers, on her side, staring at the wall. I should have been there with her in the canned goods aisle; I was the one always trying to convince her to give our father another chance. "What the fuck. I keep thinking maybe he's changed—like he'll be pretty good for a while, but then he goes and does something like that again. It's so frustrating. I'm so sorry."

She made a noise, an indication of nothing exactly, except perhaps that she knew better.

At work on Thursday, the school social worker, Ms. A, and I had to pull one of my students out of class for a meeting. We began with a conversation about the two fights she'd instigated earlier in the week, but quickly slid into her anxiety, how dumb she felt, more anxiety, insomnia, her diagnoses of ADHD and bipolar disorder, how she hadn't been taking her medicine.

I made a strategic decision to share. "You know, I'm going to tell you something: my sister is bipolar too. And even though she doesn't always like to take her meds, she takes them anyway because she knows that if she didn't, she wouldn't be okay."

I didn't tell her that even on meds, Emily was still not okay. The person in my house was not my sister—she was closed off, unopinionated, too quiet.

Our mother treated us to manicures on Friday, the last night of Emily's visit. I chose a deep shade of yellow for my fingernails. Emily chose aquamarine. On Saturday, before her flight, we went to the Louisiana Crawfish Festival in St. Bernard Parish. We ate gooey, buttery crawfish bread and rode the carnival swings: purple plastic chairs suspended above striped tents and pavement. I had then the same feeling I have now as I write: dropped stomach, unable to see straight. I asked her about her medicine while we were waiting in line for the ride. She said her doctors were working it out. She said it would be okay. I got nauseous, stood over a toilet, and hoped to vomit. Dropped her off at the airport. Took a nap. Met JK for dinner in a narrow French Quarter alley. The restaurant was beside the office of an attorney and across from an art gallery. We sat in metal chairs beneath tall potted palms and a strip of clear sky and ordered rosé sangria. I took a sip—sharp and sweet. "It's such a relief to not have to work so fucking hard to carry a conversation."

JK raised her glass. "Cheers! You're free!"

I drank to your departure because your depressed visit had been so draining. Four days later, you were dead.

PART 3

SOMEONE OR TWO, EARLY ON, sold me on the hope that my sister's suicide was a bad thing that happened that was going to make me stronger. It was how I got through the first nine months: imagining whenever I was anxious, sad, mad, or a general mess that I was learning how to be a bigger, better me.

But by the end of January, after two months of travel, it had become clear that grief was only melting down my moral veneer—the one I'd thought I'd carefully lacquered years earlier so that I could be the good version of myself: kind, calm, patient. In Thailand I often felt small, lost, unsure. I was quick to become impatient, irrational, irritable, mean, petty—to direct my disproportionate distress at myself and J, the only other person I knew within many thousands of miles. I slept fitfully. I had a warped and continual sense that what I said and did was bad, hurtful, offensive. I could not handle changes to plans. My brain moved too slowly, processed too thoroughly, wanted to explore all the intricacies of every possible next step before any decisions were made. Wanted to find some semblance of certainty in spite of the knowledge that it exists only in trace quantities, with illusory qualities. Wanted to know what I was up against.

Sometimes, on bus or train rides, I put on headphones and a playlist to reset, to give a soundtrack to the rubber trees and rice paddies and pineapple stands that sat outside while my mind wandered to my sister. Sometimes, too, I leaned my head against the window and cried. I was trying to forgive myself; I was trying to be gentle—I knew it was what I was supposed to do. Still, the better part of me believed it would be far easier to die than to keep trying.

For most of February, J and I were on an island within an island created by the eruption of a supervolcano many tens of thousands of years ago—Samosir, in Sumatra, Indonesia. It was beautiful: verdant mountains and tall, thin waterfalls, terraced green rice paddies carved into hills, intricate Toba Batak houses with steeply pitched roofs made from sugar palm fiber thatch, street-roaming water buffalo, sunsets that turned the sky electric pink and blue.

One afternoon, it was pouring rain. To pass the time, I sat outside the guesthouse where we were staying, drank coffee, smoked a clove cigarette, and read *The Week* magazine. When the rain let up a bit, I went back to our room and lay down, suddenly deeply melancholy. J sat down on the edge of the bed. I told him, "Please leave me alone." Said it made it harder, to be around him—he was always fine, and I was always thinking about Emily.

J's face fell. "I'm sorry. I think about her too. I just don't say anything. I don't know what to say. I am afraid of making it worse for you."

I sat up and moved my body beside his. "No, please tell me. It helps to hear that. I want to know."

J turned his head to meet my eager gaze, then turned away and stared straight ahead. "Well, it's the same kind of thing everyone wonders: what else I could have done, or what I should have done differently. What I think about most often is that time I visited her, you know, right after she got out of the hospital last January. I had my guitar with me, and I played for her—I thought maybe it would help cheer her up a little or something. And I— It just, it was just what had been stuck in my head. We'd just watched that Coen brothers' movie *Inside Llewyn Davis*—you remember?"

He blinked back tears as he recounted the song's title, wondering if he'd been thoughtless, had chosen wrong in singing: "Hang me, oh hang me / I'll be dead and gone." How much attention had Emily paid to the lyrics: "Wouldn't mind the hanging / But the layin' in a grave so long, poor boy"? Had he somehow planted a seed?

I gave J a hug, grateful for his vulnerability, and told him I loved him and that I understood. But I felt shaky. Almost eleven months had passed since my sister's death. That there might still be more to discover hadn't occurred to me. And why hadn't J been more thoughtful? And why had he waited so long to tell me? The questions were futile, I knew. But I wanted so badly to place my sadness outside myself, to assign blame, to be angry instead of in pain.

Our third month of travel came to a close in New South Wales. Our flight landed on the morning of Emily's birthday. There was heavy rain. We drank flat whites in a nearby coffee shop, biding the time until we could check in to our hotel and take a nap. In the afternoon, the sun came out, so we walked: past the bright-red flowers of the Royal Botanic Garden and the white peaks of the Sydney Opera House like great, unflappable sails above the blue-green waters of the Sydney Harbour. Past Hyde Park's grand avenue, flanked by lamp posts and benches and Hill's weeping fig trees. Past the twin stone spires of a vast cathedral. As we were heading back to our hotel, a gray-haired man in graying sneakers, a purple T-shirt, and faded jeans stopped us on the sidewalk.

"Are you interested in going to the special exhibit at the Art Gallery of New South Wales? I just went. It's called *Pop to Popism*, really great stuff in there. Warhol, Lichtenstein, Hockney. The ticket was $20, but I'll give it to you for half the price. I'm sure it'll work if you say you were already in there and you're reentering."

"Oh—no thanks—we're actually headed to get some lunch," J said. I could hear in his voice that he felt a bit skeptical.

"Here—just take the ticket, then. You can give it to someone else if you don't use it," the man said. He handed the ticket to J, who said thanks, then turned to me.

"Do you want to go?"

The museum was right behind us. "Yeah, I think I'd like to. Do you?"

"No, that's all right. Go ahead. Take your time. It's nice out. I'll hang outside," he said.

"Okay, I'll be quick. Let's meet at the entrance to the museum in twenty minutes."

I hadn't been sure what to do with my sister's birthday—the first one for which she was no longer living—but an art museum felt right enough. Emily was the creative one in our family; she understood color, lines, shapes, texture. She paid attention to these details. During the winter break of my junior year of college, her last year of high school, our mother and stepfather had taken me, Emily, and Ches to DC. We visited Smithsonian museums, ate Ethiopian food with our hands, and used our tongues to clean specks of hot doughnut glaze from our lips.

In the National Portrait Gallery, a city-block-sized building full of art, Emily and I wandered off on our own through grandiose halls filled with portraits of presidents and sculptures of gods, peacocks made of stained glass and cupids made of bronze. Emily wore one earring and a green knitted cap over straightened hair, carried a sketchbook and kept a scarf wrapped round her neck. She pointed out a portrait: oil paint on linen taller than both of us. We walked right up to the canvas and saw small, concentric circles of color, like a cross between Josef Albers and Georgia O'Keeffe.

"Now take ten giant steps back," Emily instructed, as if playing a children's game. Bill Clinton's face came into focus. "Isn't that so cool? Actually, one of the coolest things about Chuck Close is that he has prosopagnosia."

"You know I have no idea what that is, right?"

Emily's voice picked up speed, which was how I knew she was excited to tell me. "It's face blindness! He can't remember faces and, actually, he can't really remember much of anything unless he sees it as two-dimensional or hears it."

"That's wild."

"I know! *And*—"

I braced myself to learn a whole lot more about this artist, which was how it went with Emily: she got obsessed with something and then wouldn't stop talking about it, like the night when my friend and I camped out in my mother's backyard. We were ten and Emily was seven and she followed us around in the dark, pelting us with facts about sharks. Even after we'd put layers of fabric between her and us—tent flap, sleeping bags—and forbid her entrance, she'd sat down on the damp grass and continued to inform us cheerfully that hammerhead sharks eat stingrays and give birth to live young.

Ten years later, I was learning that Chuck Close was paralyzed at the age of forty-eight and confined to a wheelchair and, though his style shifted slightly, he had kept painting. Emily grew more animated as she drew a connection to Henri Matisse, whose cutouts were her favorite works of art.

We continued through the museum, pausing occasionally to purse our lips, close our eyes, pretend to kiss people in frames, speak in vague accents, gesture toward landscapes, pretend to be people who know a lot.

As I wandered alone through the exhibit in Sydney, I did none of this. I experienced her absence as an inability to see, imagining how much I was missing that she would have pointed out to me.

THE FOURTH MONTH OF TRAVEL, March, was split between two farms: one on which J and I helped to train a foal, and one on which we planted garlic bulbs. In April, we drove around the southern island of New Zealand in a red campervan we bought for cheap that only died on us about once a week. At night, we'd find a place to park, pull closed the wimpy curtains, and sleep on the mattress in the back of the van; by daylight we read maps, navigated roads that wound through tunnels and vineyards and everlasting coastline, and stopped to wander as we pleased.

One afternoon, we parked by a stream and put on our backpacks, prepared to hike a long trail and camp in a public hut for the night. After about an hour of steep ascents and descents, we came to a river valley. In the middle of that yellow field, I took one misstep and rolled my ankle. I crumpled to the ground, instantly defeated. Lay in the dry grass, wrapped both hands around the injured joint, and stared at the sky while J asked where it hurt, how much it hurt, if I could move it. This man, trying his very best to support me—it almost made everything worse. I sat up, J sat next to me, and we ate the lunch we'd packed.

"How does it feel now?" he asked.

"Not great. I don't think I should push it. You keep going. I'm going to go back down to the van."

We argued briefly and gently. J was worried, wanted to take care of me, and I wanted to be alone, wanted space and quiet—indefinitely. I convinced him it was okay to continue on without me, sat still for a while, then walked very slowly, feeling free.

Once I made it back, I opened the van's back doors to the breeze, lay down, opened the novel *Open City*, and let Teju Cole's soft descriptions of birds and symphonies wash over me. I listened to the inscrutable rustle of the mouse we hadn't yet been able to catch. At some point, she poked her head out from behind a pack of AA batteries. For dinner, I drank pinot noir and ate dark chocolate and plain Cheerios. I listened to an episode of *The Moth Radio Hour* and then closely read a year's worth of text messages between my sister and me.

I analyzed what was and was not said, all of the parts where I could have been better. I mentally highlighted the repetition of "love" to show myself that it qualified as a theme. There were patterns to our exchanges: the motif of medicine and whether it should be taken, was working, was worth it. Her feelings of isolation in places both full and empty of people. She was tired, low, and overwhelmed, or happy, high, and overwhelming. I was busy, unsure, or going for a run, offering unasked for advice or platitudes or plane tickets for a visit. We told one another we believed in each other. We used the word "poop" a lot. She was frightened first by how much weight she lost while manic, then gained while depressed; I, by how much food I always seemed to be eating. I saw how it all added up in a sad way: a list of grievances and love, neither one of us writing about particular happiness. Just being and grateful to be in it together. I saw all that I did and did not miss. Saw everything that had changed and would never change and how I couldn't have done anything to change it.

The lines I kept turning over in my mind were the ones in which I described feeling stuck in my relationship with J. I'd almost forgotten I'd felt that way while Emily was still alive—I had come to associate my ambivalence about the relation- ship with the aftermath. The next morning, when J returned from his overnight solo trip, I was reading in a camping chair beside the red van, my foot propped up on the back bumper. I glanced up from my book, saw him approaching, and felt as if I'd drunk a spoiled tonic that coated my throat with baseless antipathy. I gave a tight-lipped smile. He asked how my ankle was. I answered, "Fine."

J began to tell the story of his last twenty-four hours—the three young doctors he'd shared the cabin with, the cold night, how he'd hiked the last few kilometers with a group of teenagers and their teachers who were on a field trip. As he spoke, we packed up, assumed our roles: I sat in the passen- ger seat, J drove.

I decided, then, to trick myself, to see what would happen—what my brain would do, what I could convince myself to believe. I sat facing straight ahead with J's face in my peripheral vision. Then I put my sister's face in my mind, tried to remember the curvature of her cartilage and the way her hair had lain and how her lips might be pursed or parted. And once I thought I had it, once I'd painted the picture of her, I turned to look at J and tried to see my sister there instead. When it didn't work, I felt so defeated: by the presence of the present, by the shift of her-beside-me from conceivable to not there. What I wanted more than anything was impossibility.

I LEFT J IN NEW ZEALAND IN MAY. Alone, I boarded a plane to fly the nineteen hours to the States, feeling light and free. I arrived home in time to be with my mom on Mother's Day and stayed at her house for a week. Most days I found myself in the room that was still Emily's room.

Shortly after she'd left for college, Emily's sky-blue walls—including the creamy clouds that she'd invited us to help her paint when she was eight—were repainted asparagus green and glaucous blue. Since then, though, it appeared that little had been altered. Someone had relieved the bureau's overstuffed drawers of their messes of old socks and underwear, but the ceiling-high bookshelf was still crowded with books and trinkets, including her *Calvin and Hobbes* collection, a metal water bottle she'd decorated with stickers and paint, and dried flowers in an empty glass bottle of iced AriZona green tea. Her self-portrait remained on display in its frame: Emily's face as a puzzle composed of a dozen bright colors and odd shapes, the left side's features wild, the right almost sedate.

The only things new to the room were three cardboard boxes, each large enough to serve as a hiding spot, which contained Emily's dorm room. They had been packed and shipped by strangers, then opened, then ignored.

I spent a while exploring the contents, picking up each item and admiring its solidity. Though I was not quite holding my breath, I felt jittery—eager to encounter something, anything, recognizable, and hopelessly curious about the origin of everything that was not. Each new object I touched held the promise of connection to my sister, but it all smelled like vitamins: calcium, iron, vitamin C, multipurpose women's. A sickening scent of attempt, of abandonment, of health gone sour, gone stale, gone unused, gone and useless.

It wasn't Emily. She was sweat and bacteria and the occasional use of deodorant or gardenia solid perfume.

I only took one thing from one box: a kid-sized fleece jacket printed with bluish crabs. I brought it with me to the sleepaway camp in western North Carolina where I'd previously spent two college summers. There, I was surrounded by waxy rhododendron leaves, the dark, dense greens of spruce and fir, mountains, waterfalls, morning mist, and by night, a chorus of spring peeper chirps. It was a place where I felt safe, where I could ease into the transition back to life, to work, to structure. When I arrived in late May, the mornings were cold, so I often wore the fleece. Other camp counselors complimented the jacket and wanted to know where I'd gotten it. I didn't say what I always wanted to say—what I would have said four years earlier, when I was twenty-one, when I'd last worked there: "It's my sister's." It wasn't worth it to risk the confusion of past and present: I might next have to say, "Actually, it *was* my sister's." Instead, I said I found it lying around my parents' house.

One of my duties that summer was to drive groups of campers to waterfalls in a white twelve-passenger van. Before each trip, I was required to conduct a safety check: turn on the headlights, then the high beams, then both turn signals; honk the horn, put a foot on the brake, pop the hood, and check the engine oil. I'd tick off all the boxes on the paper form, then write in the date.

At some point in July as I followed this procedure, I looked down at my watch and saw that it was the twenty-sixth. I hadn't realized. For the past fifteen months, each twenty-sixth had haunted me, hardening the truth that I was still here, one month further from Emily. But in the fantasy land of summer camp, time seemed to pass differently. I had stopped keeping track.

That evening, I had a night off. Instead of going out for a drink with the other counselors, I lay in my bed with my iPad, scrolling social media. I stopped at a post my mother had shared: "Wait. What? Didn't even know this existed. Oh, Emily . . ." and a link to a two-minute video titled "Nature is ME."

It opened with bird tweets and upbeat, twinkly music. Little kids and adults talked about the beauty of nature in Maine. They smiled and laughed into the camera. There were stills of green zucchini and broccoli, pink flowers and radishes, yellow carrots. Then, over a white fence in a green pasture below a sky half-covered by clouds, came a voice detached from a body: "It feels really good to just be in the dirt, be with the land. It's beautiful. Nature is me." I hadn't heard Emily's voice in over a year. I wouldn't have been sure it was hers had there not also been a shot of her face: squinted brown eyes, hair cropped close to her head, her nose ring. And her ever-tremulous hands, traces of dirt under clipped fingernails, holding up an egg-shaped red potato into which she'd carved a smiley face.

When the video ended, I got up, grabbed a nearby jar of almond butter, and unscrewed the lid. I wasn't sure what else to do. I thought about writing a letter to J. But when I'd ended the relationship, I'd forfeited that option. I had to function on my own. I had to show myself I could. I was tired of complaining anyway. I was tired in general, and it seemed like it might be better to just go to bed.

Instead, I stayed up late doing nothing, then woke up before sunrise to run eighteen miles. I didn't really have a choice—I was training for a marathon that my aunt K had proposed we run together in California in late August. I'd said yes both because I wanted to spend a weekend with her and because I thought the race would be a good test, a way to see how seventeen months of grief had tempered me.

After the sunrise run, I stretched, drenched in sweat. Layers of salt crusted the corners of my eyes. When my playlist spit out "Orange Sky," a song featured in *Away We Go* (a movie Emily and I had watched together multiple times), I tried hard not to cry. I missed my sister. Missed sitting on a couch together, laughing at the same lines in movies and sharing associations with certain songs. I wished I could reach out and touch her. I missed her voice, her smile, her skin. I missed being sisters with Emily.

The marathon coursed through Santa Rosa on an overcast morning in late August: steep hills and paved roads; grapevines arranged in neat, bright-green rows; wine cellars filled with oak barrels; shop windows; a small bridge resting over a creek so low the water barely flowed. The race was hard. As I began to feel my legs burn two and a half hours in, as I began to doubt my own body, I did what every runner does: I drew from stores of glycogen and thoughts of "this is nothing compared to what I've already gotten myself through."

And then at mile 19 a side stitch crept in and kicked my butt. It didn't really matter how many months I'd spent pushing through the pain of loss to get this far—my diaphragm didn't give a fuck. So, I moved through 7.2 more miles of not being able to breathe, and then it was finished.

Two years before I met J, I met a boy named P. I was twenty, and P was a year older than me, tall and lean with hair curled and gently blond, in his voice a hint of Southern honey. His wide-set green eyes, easy smile, and jawline made for a face that one might find in a J.Crew catalog. It was my first summer at the sleepaway camp; we worked together, and I had a crush on him. On a night off, we got quite drunk and kissed. Camp ended, and he accompanied me on my drive from North Carolina to Delaware. When we arrived at my mother's house, Emily was there. The three of us drank red wine in the kitchen and cooked spaghetti for dinner. I went back to school in Colorado, he returned to North Carolina.

Five summers later, we met again. P first made the two-hour drive from Charlotte, where he was working as an EMT, because the camp director asked him to help with an orientation training. Next, he came to see his brother, who was also on staff. Then he just kept showing up. I invited him to join me on my marathon training runs. We had conversations about the importance of community, the poison of white saviorism, the desire that we shared to feel settled somewhere. It was nice to reconnect.

Again on a night off, a few drinks in and a few months out of my relationship with J, I kissed P in the middle of a gravel pathway. I'd meant to stay alone, but I quickly slipped back into love. P hid handwritten notes between the pages of the novel I was reading and tucked secret mangoes into my tote bag. When I visited him in Charlotte, we idled in the aisles of bookshops and lay contented in his bed. It helped that he had met my sister. We decided to see where part two of this romance might lead.

When camp ended in August, I drove myself south to New Orleans with a drained bank account. I had procured temporary employment at the high school where I used to teach as a long-term substitute for a ninth-grade science teacher who had been on maternity leave. I accepted JK's offer to move into her living room, which she furnished with a bed for me. P talked about moving to New Orleans. We kept in touch via letters, emails, FaceTime calls.

All through that fall, I woke up while the morning was still dark. I might lie still and hope to fall back asleep, or I might get up and run: a few miles along the bayou, streetlamps, sunrise, an abandoned medical center brought back to life by light. Or I might drive to the New Orleans Athletic Club to swim laps. In the locker room, I'd turn away from other women as I peeled off my suit, pretending not to listen in on the conversations held in various stages of undress— something about it felt more invasive than eavesdropping on the fully clothed.

One morning, two freshly showered bodies stood together in their workday underwear speculating about how a friend of a friend had died. They concluded, through an analysis of Facebook posts, that the cause of death was most likely suicide. I felt a familiar gut punch, like I was surrounded, like my loss had me tuned in to a suicide frequency, some invisible wave that kept me all too alert to suicide's shadow forms, how they follow the living. The locker room was new, but not surprising. It was everywhere, in everything I heard and saw and read. It made

me want to tear off my ears and gouge out my eyes—the things
that led me places I didn't want to go.

After I ran or swam or stayed in bed, I'd head to one of my
part-time jobs: middle school reading intervention teacher,
babysitter, food truck cashier, nonprofit program leader, or
front desk girl at a boutique fitness studio. If it was job one, I
might be tasked with the administration of a test to seventh
graders strewn about an unused classroom. They'd stare
down long passages of text, take pencils to bubbles on blue
booklet pages, and look longingly at the door, the windows,
the ceiling. I, too, would want to leave.

On my way home, I often had to stop to get gas, and I
once impulsively bought a pack of cigarettes. On the worst
days, when I wanted to feel close to Emily, I'd sit and smoke on
my back steps in a tank top and underwear, my arms heavy,
the sky warm and blue, gray clouds moving too fast, the wind
slamming neighbors' unlatched screen doors open and shut.
My hands smelled of smoke and gasoline. No matter what I
did, I felt lost. Afraid and uncertain. Exhausted, depleted. All I
wanted was out. There was no foreseeable end.

In the evenings, I went to work again. One night, this took
the form of a meeting at a beer garden with my coworkers from
the nonprofit, string lights and sail-sized triangles of green and
white fabric above our heads. We sat in black perforated metal
chairs around a round table, drinking bottles of pale ale. My
phone rang. I checked to see who was calling, though I couldn't
really answer. I was surprised by the name on the screen: it
was A, my sister's friend. Just in case something was wrong, I
excused myself to take the call.

As soon as I said hello, words flooded out of A like she was
on the edge of something—kind of incoherent, kind of repet-
itive, more than kind of overwhelmed. She said, "I called you

because no one picked up from my list of people to call in an emergency," by which I inferred she meant if she was feeling suicidal. I paced around and around blocks of broken sidewalks and houses peeling paint; I asked questions and listened and stayed on the line until A said she felt safe. By the time we hung up, my meeting had ended.

On my walk home, I was shaken. I tried to call three different people, but none of them answered. What if I'd needed them? What then? I felt alone and afraid. For so long after Emily's death, I had been certain that each call I received was urgent. I reminded myself that it was normal to not pick up, even for me . . . And then it hit me. Maybe, in this peculiar way, I was myself again: I, too, was a person who did not always pick up.

MY MOTHER AND FATHER HAD BOTH DECIDED, separately, that the savings bonds my sister had been given over the years by various relatives would be given to me. The total was about a thousand dollars. There was no significance to this lump sum. There was nothing commemorative to spend it on. It was just the fact that she could help me out one last time—that there is something like a lottery-by-death that, in November, gave me the means to put down the safety deposit and first month's rent on a house in New Orleans with P.

To commemorate his move, we went on a date to see *Brooklyn* at the Prytania Theatre, a hundred-year-old single-screen with a redbrick facade. We splurged on popcorn. The previews played, then the movie began. No one had warned me that the love story would be tangled up in the story of a sister dying. I had never heard anyone else say the things I thought all the time, like "I'll never see her again," and "I can't believe I'm married to someone you'll never know." As I shrank, sank into my seat, I received a hand squeeze from P that I hoped was intentional.

When I'd decided to end my relationship with J, this was what I imagined would be hard. None of the men I dated after my sister's death ever quite understood how sad and lonely it feels never to be asked about Emily, how I want an excuse to talk about her. None ever quite grasped that she is the reason why I might be inexplicably sad and lonely, no matter how much time has passed. They were not around—a free pass while someone before them stuck out the worst of my grief. Stuck out so many months of tears and apologies and cruelty, distress, and jumpy reactions—jumpiness in general.

J was there through it all. He was the first person I'd called on that Wednesday when I got the news. I was outside, sitting at a maroon thermoplastic-coated picnic table by the football field. When J answered, he was on a ski lift, suspended, mid-air. His sister was next to him—she'd traveled out west for a visit. He sounded cheerful, a little out of breath.

I didn't know what to say, so I said, "Emily killed herself." There was no response. I repeated what I'd said: "She's dead. Emily is dead." He didn't seem to understand. Then he did. He reached the top of the lift and forgot where he was—his body had a job to do but he could not move. He had to be pulled onto the mountain by his sister and the lift operator.

He flew east the next day. I was in bed by the time he got to my mother's house; he lay down beside me and held me. We kissed so softly, then the touch became urgent, then I couldn't let go. From below three layers of fascia surfaced the first gasp of heartache. We made the most literal love: to fill what was empty, to mend what was broken, to relieve the paralytic pain of irrational loss.

IN JANUARY, J MAILED ME his band's finally finished album, the one he'd moved from New Orleans to Colorado two years earlier to write. I opened the slim package as soon as it arrived, ran my fingers over the matte sleeve of the cover, read the credits printed on the back and saw that it was dedicated to his friend's father, who'd died when we were fresh out of college, and to Emily.

I was afraid of the album—afraid of what memories or feelings the music might evoke. I didn't listen to it until Emily's birthday at the end of February. I went for a drive and put it in my car's CD player and turned up the volume. What I felt was a longing. What I felt was so far from J and the rest of the band. Though they were also my friends, I hadn't been in touch with any of them. I feared that because I'd hurt J, they might all be done with me.

In reality, they were probably just busy, but I was too scared to find out for sure. All my friends felt far away. It was my job, I knew, to ask them to be closer. But I wanted my sister to be closer, and everyone and everything else was not her.

The closest I came to Emily was in my dreams. I liked best the ones in which both of us knew she had died but we interacted as if nothing had happened. I could hear her voice, her words out of her mouth, and it felt like I hadn't forgotten. In one such dream, she was upset about a note she intended to give to our sixth-grade teacher. It was written on a hot-pink Post-it, and she thought it was dumb, or maybe weird. It was neither. It was brilliant—an experiment of images and questions typical of my sister—but she could be neither consoled nor convinced. In another, I walked into my classroom unprepared and couldn't get my students under control; everyone needed my attention, yet no one would listen to me. Suddenly I was home in Delaware with a tattoo across my back: two words in bold black ink. As I looked in my closet for an outfit to wear to work, I felt anxious and thought, "Oh, I'll sleep in bed next to Emily tonight—that will make me feel better."

My alarm went off at 5:38 a.m. I snoozed through it for thirteen minutes, just barely making it to a six o'clock yoga class at the studio where I worked. The teacher instructed us to begin with a meditation: find a place in our bodies that felt congested, constricted—imagine a bird in it. I placed a little brown house finch next to my heart and felt it try to flap its wings beneath the cage of my ribs where there was no space to stretch.

When the class ended, I sprayed my mat with eucalyptus-scented water, wiped it down with a hand towel, and slowly, evenly rolled it up. I put on my hoodie and sandals, then looked at my phone. There was a text from D, Emily's childhood friend. A thoughtful message: "I know this week must be hard." He said he was thinking of me and my whole family.

From deep in my stomach, an irritation uncoiled itself. Must this week be hard? It was late March, but I was still getting out of bed, still exercising, still eating. I still smiled and forced myself to bathe. To do so had been slow, laborious. But the listlessness was all in my head. It had to be. It had been two years and I wanted to be fine already. I had four jobs and no spare time or energy for grief. If I acknowledged its power, it would destroy me.

Three days later, on the second anniversary of Emily's death, I woke up at 5:30 a.m., safety pinned a Tyvek bib to a tank top, and drove to Lafayette Square to run the Crescent City Classic, an annual 10k race. The breaking day was gray, the square was green, and the air was at 89 percent humidity. In a sea of people wearing superhero costumes and tutus and bunny ears, I ran from the Superdome through the Central Business District, along Decatur Street, past Café du Monde and the French Market, then up to City Park on Esplanade Avenue.

Postrace, everything felt light and bright: endorphins and beer and zydeco music, mimosas and chips and guacamole, holding hands with P, a friend of a friend's backyard party, the sun that had come out, a game of celebrity. Maybe I was supposed to feel sad, but I felt lucky.

I WAS ONCE TAUGHT THAT in Eastern writing it is common for stories to move in spirals while Western academics like straight, narrow lines. I can admit that there is refuge in the tragic: a freedom from the expectation of a clean, continuous narrative. When I interviewed for a full-time position as a ninth-grade reading teacher and was asked to explain the gap in my résumé, all I'd had to say was "My sister died," and I received a round of I'm-so-sorrys before they hurried on to the next question. I didn't have to list the whole sequence: how I left a job and a city I love, lived at home for a summer, escaped to Maine for a fall, wandered the world for five months with my boyfriend, broke up with my boyfriend, moved back to the States, worked at a sleepaway camp for a summer, entered into a new relationship, returned to New Orleans, pieced together part-time work for a year, and worried daily about the bills I couldn't pay.

When I was offered the job, I accepted. To do so was practical and safe—it meant health insurance and steady pay—and also the opposite of what I wanted to do.

Going back to school to give writing a real shot wasn't a goal I'd said aloud a lot—maybe once to J and once to P—but it also wasn't out of the blue. In fourth grade, my class was given an assignment to fast-forward twenty-five years, accept an award, and share our professional biographies. My classmates were soccer players, actors of the year, or scientists.

One of my friends was Irish dancer of the year. I declared that, as "author of the year" at the age of thirty-five, I had gone to a college in Colorado (the one I actually went to), then moved to Boston and wrote a Newbery Award–winning children's book called *Doodles*. In reality, from the age of ten until my sister died when I was twenty-three, I rarely wrote, except for sporadic journal entries.

A year into sharing my writing, I received an email from a friend that planted a seed. The subject line: "Direction?"

> Hey, Becca. I was thinking of you again this morning, and wondering if you'd thought to write a book about your and Emily's relationship, one that might extend its domain to the relevant societal issues. Is that where all this is heading? (I think you're a good enough writer and a strong enough person to do it, and do it well.)

Six months later, I wrote back.

> This may not be true, but what I suspect is that the reason it has taken me so long to write back to you (besides working nonstop for the last four months) is because your note terrified me. Still does, a bit. I have thought to turn my writing into something long-form, substantial. Here is the truth: I want so badly to try to do this that it scares the shit out of me. It makes me cry.

Still, I didn't know if my sister would approve. That's not true—I knew. But telling myself what Emily would have said was not the same as what I needed to hear: her voice, relief from chaos, this paralyzing weight, how each decision made after her death couldn't matter any more or less.

During professional development, in late July, I sat at a table with my grade-level team. A bowl of fortune cookie–sized pieces of paper containing icebreaker questions was passed around. We were instructed to choose one each. I pulled: "If you had one (and only one) wish come true this year, what would it be?"

I couldn't say "Emily" to this group of strangers. I didn't want it to be the answer, but I didn't have a choice. So, I pulled another slip of paper: "If you could change one thing about yourself, what would it be?" The answer came to me immediately: How hard it is for me to verbalize my thoughts. (How they trip and fall as they descend brain to tongue. How my tone comes out mean. How I'd rather sit through a silent retreat in a torture chamber, stuck with needles again and again, unable to scream, let alone speak, than attempt to say out loud what I really think or feel or want or need.)

Later, we all attended a trauma-informed instruction training. The facilitator asked us to imagine our own "safe space," whether real or imagined: Where was it? Who, if anyone, was there? We sat in silence. At first, my mind drew only scribbles in black ink that felt more frightening than safe. I arrived at the Mediterranean Sea, on a gray morning shoreline covered in shells I'd once walked along, and Emily was with me. Our arms were linked, and I could almost drink the comfort that poured from her body.

The facilitator asked for volunteers to share, scanning the circular arrangement of teachers in student-sized chairs. After a moment of hesitation, one woman said, "I'll do it." She described an imaginary house deep in the woods, far, far from other people except for her brother—when she pictured the house, her brother was there.

At the session's conclusion, I approached her. "Hey, I just wanted to tell you that I appreciated you sharing earlier. You and your brother must be close?"

"Yeah, he's my best friend," she said.

"That's awesome," I said. I had been hoping he, too, might be dead. "Do you get to see him often?"

She proceeded to tell me where he lives and what he does for a living. As I listened, I lapsed into embarrassment. How obvious I must have been: desperate to connect with someone who, like me, maybe only wanted a person to always be there once they could no longer possibly be.

My classroom was entirely robin's-egg blue, except for one tall wall of windows. Desks were arranged in pairs that faced the projection screen at the front. A whiteboard that ran the length of the wall opposite the windows led to a reading nook made up of a rug, bookshelves, and pillows. At the back of the room was a Chromebook cart and a teacher's desk. The decor comprised of posters: my four vague class rules ("Be nice; Be productive; Be a good listener; Do not quit"), three sets of student-generated community guidelines (one per class), visual prompts for skills like metacognition and annotation, and quotes I'd hoped my students would find inspirational ("When you're trying to motivate yourself, appreciate the fact that you're even thinking about making a change. And as you move forward, allow yourself to be good enough."—Dr. Alice Domar).

One morning, around 7:10, I walked into my classroom carrying three tote bags. I crossed the room to drop them on the chair behind the teacher's desk, which mainly served as storage, took a sip of my iced coffee, and glanced at my phone. There was an email from Emily. I felt panic in my chest, a momentary slip in reason, a rush of hope, then confusion. Though it must have lasted only milliseconds, it felt like decades before rationality kicked in and dismissed the notion: the message couldn't be from my sister.

Indeed, the email was from the school's college counselor. I read it and continued to sip my coffee. The first bell rang at 7:42 a.m. I put my phone away. The day proceeded as usual: I said good morning as my students trickled in, taught my first-period class, then my second, then met with my advisory group of goofy, well-meaning ninth-grade boys, then grabbed my lunch from one of the totes. It was 11:04 a.m. I took a bite of salad, appreciating the moment of calm before students inevitably showed up at my door with trays of food, asking if they could eat in my room.

Every other day, I had a planning period after lunch— usually I graded or prepared for the next day's lesson, but sometimes I changed into shorts and sneakers and snuck off campus. I would run a few miles between streetcar tracks on the St. Charles Avenue neutral ground or do a loop through Audubon Park, past mansions and playgrounds and flocks of ducks and games of Frisbee, past college students lying beside open textbooks on blankets in the grass. At the end of the run, I used paper towels from the faculty bathroom to wipe the sweat from my body, changed back into my work clothes, and proceeded to teach my last class until the 3:10 p.m. bell.

If there wasn't a grade-level or all-staff meeting after school, I'd most often stay anyway: either to lead a practice for a youth running club or because there was still so much more work to do. One afternoon, I found myself in a poorly lit storage closet full of books in search of possible additions to my classroom library appropriate for struggling readers. Teacher A walked by and asked what I'd found in there. Teacher B stopped in to ask Teacher A a question. Then the three of us stood surveying class sets of *Speak*, *Middle Passage*, *Things Fall Apart*, *The Bluest Eye*, *Salvage the Bones*, *Brave New World*—and an impromptu book club discussion ensued. Teacher B lamented her lack of interest in Toni Morrison's writing, her hesitancy to read about the fictional traumatizing of children, her penchant, as a reader, for the lighthearted. Teacher A shared

regret over her decision to read *Crime and Punishment* while caring for her sick mother—the parallel gravity of the story and
real life felt like more than she could handle. I then said that I
was grateful to have finished reading one of my favorite books,
Men We Reaped, a month before my sister died; I might not have
had the capacity to absorb Jesmyn Ward's grief otherwise.

ON A TUESDAY IN LATE SEPTEMBER, I was already worn out by my students by the time I got to sit down for lunch. I typed in my phone's passcode, intending to let myself zone out.

A little red dot indicated I had a message on a social media app. I checked it compulsively. What I read was unexpected: a college classmate of mine had placed himself in front of an Amtrak train. Though I hadn't known Ari well, I immediately recalled his wide smile and red hair, the sound of his voice, his warm presence, his passion for rock climbing.

I had no time. I had a meeting. I stood up, phone and keys in hand, and walked down the hall to a colleague's classroom and sat at a desk. I nodded through a conversation to which I could not contribute, flooded with the knowledge of how it feels to lose a person, with questions that felt only wrong: Had anyone considered how this news might feel for me? Was anyone wondering if I was okay?

My colleague asked me a question.

"I'm really sorry," I said. I liked this teacher, and I didn't want to disappoint her. "I thought I'd be fine, but right before we met, I found out someone I know from college died. I'm having a hard time focusing." I began to cry, not because I was especially sad about losing him but because no one I'd known personally had died by suicide in the last two and a half years. I was taken aback by the intimacy with which I felt connected to this particular death.

My colleague insisted I leave early—she'd arrange for someone to cover my last class. I drove home, parked my car, unlocked the door to the house I shared with P, set down my tote bags, walked straight to the kitchen. I was not hungry. I reflexively spread butter on a piece of pita bread, scarcely conscious of chewing. Climbed into bed, covers over my head, shaking quietly.

For weeks I was beset by a visceral loss of control. A hatred of everything that I put into my body, a coldness that caused me to stiffen at being touched. I felt like I was unraveling. When P tried to hug me, I was unable to explain my reaction, and he was unable to guess what was wrong. I couldn't make my skin stop crawling no matter how hard I scratched. How badly I wanted to rip myself in half.

During fall break in October, I took a trip west to visit my friend AJ in Portland. We journaled side by side in silence, went on runs, went on walks. We hiked a leaf-covered trail surrounded by yellow-green ferns and moss and the wispy cloud-kissed tips of mountains. The Columbia River was wide and blue below.

On the last night of my visit, we smoked a joint, lay on AJ's couch, and spooned ice cream straight from the pint. AJ listened as I sorted out my thoughts: it was becoming clearer to me that I wanted to leave the classroom. Although I sincerely loved my students, the job was exhausting, the pay disproportionate to the work, and any picture of myself in it for another year was barely visible.

"That makes a lot of sense. Teaching is hard! Do you have any ideas about what you might like to do instead?"

I said yes, actually—and during the long flight back to New Orleans, I began to draft a personal statement for a graduate school application. Getting in to a creative writing

MFA program was very far from given, but to apply none-theless felt like some small taking of life into my own hands.

At 7 a.m. on Christmas Eve, P and I got into his old Honda Accord. His car had no air-conditioning, but it did have heat, unlike mine, and was therefore the seasonally appropriate vehicle for the long drive to Atlanta.

P picked at the sleep crusted in his eyes before putting his hands on the wheel. In a deep voice and British accent, he announced, "Here we go—to Mordor!"

I laughed. "To do what?"

"Go see my parents." He put on his orange plastic sunglasses and a Chance the Rapper album, and off we went.

Through Louisiana, Mississippi, and Alabama, we made a game out of counting the billboards that seemed to appear every few miles advertising the same personal injury lawyer. At some point, to keep myself amused, I stuck my legs through the sleeves of my pullover fleece and said, "Look at my blanket!"

P shook his head with a smile and took a bite of a banana. I giggled and took a bite of roasted seaweed.

After eight hours, we finally arrived. His family's home was festive, filled with assorted nutcrackers, ceramic Santa plates, poinsettias, bowls of red and green peanut M&M's, six stockings hung above the fireplace, and a very tall tree. That night we went out for Chinese food with his parents and three younger brothers. When we got back to their house, his mother produced a menorah and candles she'd gotten just for me. I was touched by her thoughtfulness; I lit the candles and recited the three prayers for the first night of Hanukkah.

On Christmas morning, we opened presents and ate a big breakfast. In the afternoon, I went for a ten-mile run. For dinner there was ham and wine and beer and a game of Monopoly.

On the twenty-sixth, P and I drove four more hours to Nashville, where we were meeting my mother, stepfather, Ches, and Bubbie. The house they'd rented was newly constructed: concrete, glass, and corrugated metal, tall and sleek and indistinguishable from all the rest on the street. Save for the Buddha statuette sitting in meditation by the entrance. We had the code to the front door, so we brought in our bags, picked out a bedroom, and lay down to rest.

When my family arrived, my stepfather called out "Hello!" in a voice both loud and merry. I came downstairs, P trailing me, to see the four of them setting down a cooler, several suitcases, and several brown paper grocery bags.

"Hi! How was the drive? What is all that?" I asked as I initiated a round of hugs.

My mother pointed at the cooler. "I packed everything in our fridge that would've gone bad while we were here"— she gestured toward the paper bags—"and brought our Hanukkah decorations!"

I gave a skeptical smile. Walked over to the refrigerator to help by unloading the cooler while my mother laid out the decorations on a table by the fireplace. There were children's books titled "Hanukkah," dreidels, a blue-and-white teddy bear, a mug imprinted with colorful candles, a very old paperboard "Happy Hanukkah" banner, and menorahs variously rendered in crayon, marker, or glitter. Many of the construction paper collages were the work of preschool-aged Emily. The sun went down. We placed four candles in a silver menorah shaped like a tree. We recited the blessings and lit the candles left to right.

The morning before we departed, P and I stood with my mother in a long line to buy biscuits from a trendy brunch restaurant she'd read about. We returned to the house with three flavors of jam (blackberry lemon, harvest strawberry, summer peach) and a dozen squares of flour and butter infused with air, then all gathered around the dining table to eat.

This was, apparently, an appropriate time to discuss Emily's remains—a topic about which I'd heard nothing over the course of the last thirty-three months. My mother told me I was entitled to a portion of my sister's ashes. My step-father talked about their plans to spread the rest near the farm in Maine where Emily had worked. They kept calling it "her happy place." As I listened my body buzzed. I felt ravaged, like a tomato plant eaten alive by the piercing-sucking mouthparts of hundreds of aphids. I wanted to scream. Well before she died, Emily and I had agreed that the concept was warped: to attach happiness to place seemed like a mistake, an invitation to be miserable everywhere else, undue emphasis on one spot and one emotion, pressure to feel a certain way, the implicit denial that it all might wash away.

I stood up and stared at a patch of light on the floor. My stepfather asked me, "What do you think you'll do with yours?"

The delicacy with which he presented the question made my body stiffen with disgust. As if I would break just by thinking about it. As if I didn't think about her already. As if at the invocation of her name milky rivers would flow from every pore and my skin would turn sour and my blood would curdle. Will you eat them? Will you spread them over your body? Will you plant them in the ground so a million new little sister sprouts can rise up out of the earth?

I said, "I don't know," and went upstairs.

THE NEXT TIME I SAW MY FAMILY, just a few weeks later, my mother and I almost immediately got into a fight. I'd flown up for two days because all she wanted for her birthday was for us all to be together. When I entered the house carrying a bouquet of sunflowers, I knew something was off. (As Ches once said, "I know what her mood is from the moment I enter the house, even if she's sitting silently in another room.") My mother ignored the flowers and hardly said hello, let alone hugged me. Unsure of what I'd done wrong, I, in turn, withdrew. The table was set for dinner. Instead of addressing the tension, we sat down with Ches and my stepfather and feigned politeness.

After the meal, Ches and I cleared the table and loaded the dishwasher. It had gotten late, and I was tired. I'd woken up very early that morning to travel here, and I didn't know what my mother wanted from me. I said good night, then retreated to my bedroom.

Fifteen minutes later, there was a knock on the door; my mother said we needed to talk. Head on my pillow, I glared at the door and wished she would go away. I didn't have the energy to engage, but I came out of the room anyway. Crossed my arms and followed her downstairs, through the living room, into the sunroom. I sat in the spot on the sofa farthest from her and hugged a pillow to my chest.

"I had a sense that you didn't want to come home this weekend," she said. "I'm asking you, did you feel that way?"

"I don't know how to answer that question, Mom."

"Did you want to come here or not?"

"If I didn't want to come here, I wouldn't have come here," I said. "What is going on? Where is this coming from?"

After an interminable back-and-forth, my mother finally told me that after reading the most recent writing I'd posted online, she felt she needed to protect herself. She disagreed with my interpretation of her actions. She did not want to open up to me, but she did want to set the record straight.

What came out next were feelings I maybe could have guessed at but had never actually been told. Like how my mother never believed Emily would kill herself—she'd thought Emily's relationships to people were strong enough to keep her here; like how she would always regret that she did not follow her instinct to fly out to Colorado to check on Emily that winter and instead abided by the message my father had relayed from Emily not to come; like how painful it was that the last time my mother saw Emily was at Thanksgiving, when they were not getting along; like how awful it was that I'd kept hidden from her the fact that my father was with us in New Orleans and had gotten an unwitting last visit six days before Emily died; like how mad she was at the family court judge who had granted our father joint custody and her fantasies, after Emily died, of finding that judge and telling him what happened. ("Not that I blame your dad—I don't.")

It was the most I'd heard any member of my family speak about the constitution of their grief since the interlude between death and funeral. Beyond the perfunctory mentions of Emily (birthday, death day, remember whens), no one had shared with me what they felt. To be fair, I hadn't

asked. I never felt sure of how, or when, or where to. Nor did
I share with them, besides what I wrote and shared publicly.

"I'm so sorry, Mom—I had no idea."

"In my mind, the less I tell you, the less I put you in the
middle of things and risk upsetting you. I know we have a
history of this, but I don't want to be protected from the truth
anymore," she said. "I want us to have a relationship—I'm
afraid of losing you."

"You're not going to lose me."

My mother's face scrunched into tears. "Becca, I didn't
say it was rational. I already lost a child. Okay?"

"Okay." I got up from my seat and walked over. "Okay."
I bent my body over hers for a hug. "Okay. I love you. Thank
you for talking to me."

"It would have been really easy for me to just go to bed
upset instead of making you come talk with me. I'm really
glad you came up today. It means a lot to me. Thank you for
the beautiful flowers. I should have hugged you. I'm sorry. I
shouldn't have held back."

In the morning, my mother and I sat on stools at the kitchen
table, drinking coffee in our pajamas. My stepfather was riding the stationary bike in the basement, and Ches was still in
bed. Through the large picture window above the sink, the
day appeared dreary: overcast sky, a few brown leaves clinging to otherwise bare branches, half-frozen patches of mud.

"I want to give you some of Emily's ashes before you
leave," said my mother. I shrugged my consent, though it
wasn't wholly a question. She got up from her seat and left
the room; I wasn't sure where she'd gone or what would happen next. My father and stepmother had a solid, somber urn
on their mantel, and they'd given me a dash of Emily in a
slim hourglass-shaped vial on a chain that could be worn

as a necklace. It was something I appreciated having, but knew I'd never wear. It lay beneath pens and bookmarks in a ceramic cup made by the friend to whom I'd given Emily's art supplies. The cup sat on the slightly wobbly bedside table that J had made for me from scrap wood. I usually forgot the necklace was there.

When my mother came back into the kitchen, she was carrying a clear plastic bag of what looked like discolored flour. She set it down on the table, and I lifted it up with both hands. Its weight was surprising. How heavy, how substantial, a burned up body can be. I slowly pulled the plastic cable zip tie from the opening; it was the closest I'd been to my sister since I said goodbye and see you soon, when I dropped her off at the airport in New Orleans.

I'd had a chance to see the body before it was cremated, but I didn't take it. I did not want my last memory of my sister to be a mass of muscle, bone, and flesh without warmth or texture: bumpy arms, calloused fingers, soft wrists.

At the funeral service, as I stood beside my father, poised to receive all the hands anxious to be shaken, he pulled out a small white square from an inner pocket of his suit jacket. "Did you see Emmy?" he asked.

Before I could turn my head away or say no, no, no thanks, I was confronted with a passport-sized photo of her lifeless face: lids shut, skin ashen, lips blue.

The ashes in front of me forced a different sort of reckoning. I wasn't sure if the dust meant something to me, whether it was supposed to. The sentiment was a blank, the absence of some recognition or connection that I wished would come over me. I began to open kitchen drawers, to look for a suitable container. Something not too large, with a lid that wouldn't come undone accidentally. I found an empty plastic pepper shaker, into which I scooped my sister. To my mother, I joked, "I guess I'll just sprinkle some of Emily's ashes on top of my meals for the next year."

This made her laugh, which I was grateful for. The truth was I didn't know what I would do. I snapped the lid on the shaker and placed it in a ziplock bag in my suitcase, and when the TSA agent pulled it out and held it up to the light as I went through security, I wondered what he was thinking. I'm sure he'd seen stranger things.

THE LAST DAY OF WORK before Mardi Gras break was a day of professional development that didn't begin until 9 a.m. I woke up early to take a yoga class JK was teaching. Afterward, we sat in the middle of the sidewalk on Magazine Street and drank fancy juices, grateful for the luxury of time, the morning sun, the warm concrete, the smooth glass bottles, the bright, tart liquid.

Professional development involved stiff chairs at round tables in an open auditorium, and all I wanted to do was move. I'd made it to the last two hours before the weeklong break when, at 1:31 p.m., my phone buzzed in my pocket. I pulled it out and checked it under the table—an email from one of the MFA programs to which I had applied. *Not accepted.*

At 1:32 p.m. my phone buzzed again with an email from J.

After eighteen mostly silent months, when a mutual friend died in a ski accident, I'd reached out to him. What bitterness lingered, lessened, and we began to dance around friendship by exchanging occasional messages. This one contained a recent recording of a song he'd written during the fall we spent together in Maine after Emily died.

I excused myself to the bathroom to listen. The opening was ominous, like a haunted house theme song, then there was a clear guitar rift before J asked, "Will she ever go back to the way she was?" The mournful fun house vocals, the quick tempo that occasionally slowed, and the oscillation between dense instrumentals and space brought to mind both the Allman Brothers and Pink Floyd. I stayed in the bathroom stall and played the song again: in parallel verses, J was singing to Emily about me ("Well I know that she's not you / but she's here and she, too, has that same dark rhythm / pushing through") and to me about Emily ("Yes I know that she's not you / but when she was here, she, too, had that same old rhythm / pushing through").

The frustration and care in his voice, his very wondering, served as a balm. It also stung. Not a sting but something deeper—a pull. A twisting. A scraping off of a scab too soon, combined with the rejection, combined with Emily's approaching birthday. Not being good enough, not getting in, being left behind, her leaving.

By mid-March, I'd heard back from all three graduate schools to which I'd applied: one rejection, one acceptance, and one wait-list placement. The acceptance was to an MFA program that allowed me to stay in New Orleans. The proximity was convenient, and, as my only option, it seemed good enough.

Then, on a Saturday in mid-April, I got a call notifying me that I'd been accepted off the wait-list at a program on the North Carolina coast. I didn't have long to give an answer, but I wanted first to sit in on a class or two, and that weekend P and I happened to be a few hours west of the school, visiting friends from our sleepaway camp. I borrowed a laptop to try to figure out the logistics: I'd need to rent a car to drive across the state, plus buy a return ticket from a different airport on a different date. To do so was prohibitively expensive. One of our friends volunteered to use the credit card points he'd accrued to book a new flight home for me. His offer was generous and genuine and challenged my illusion of self-sufficiency. But if I didn't accept the gift, I wouldn't be able to afford to visit, and to visit felt important, so I did.

When I arrived in New Orleans after the two extra days away, I knew what I wanted to do. P and I discussed what it would mean for us. He was supportive. The next day, I sent in my deposit. In three months, I would move.

With the knowledge that I was again leaving the city I loved, I began to soak it all in: the sun and the heat, breakfast tacos from Pagoda Café and falafel from 1000 Figs, runs on Tuesday nights with the 504th Run Crew, unhurried Sundays at Sólo Espresso or Courtyard Brewery.

One late April morning, I woke up early to walk along the bayou before work. As the sun spread golden swaths across the sky, I passed ducks with their heads underwater, eight geese in a lopsided V, a butterfly who lay perfectly still, chirping squirrels, and occasional joggers. I found myself thinking about one my students. All week she had been closed off and moody, unable to focus. When I'd asked her what was going on, she informed me of the approaching anniversary of her grandfather's death.

In class that afternoon, instead of using her computer to work on the assignment I'd given, this student pulled up a local news report about her grandfather: a fifty-six-year-old man stabbed to death by his nephew on Piety Street and then wrapped in a blanket, stuffed in trash bags, and hidden in a shed. She sat and stared at year-old photos of neighbors, sidewalks, yellow tape, her mother's face buried in tissues. Then she closed the laptop, folded her arms on the desk, and laid down her head.

"I have an idea," I said to her, as soft and gentle as I could. "Do you want to hear it?"

She turned her head just enough that I could see the lids of her eyes open in the direction of my voice. Because she was stubborn even at baseline, I took this as a yes.

"What if you wrote a letter to your papa? You could do it while the rest of the class works on the assignment, if you wanted."

"What do you mean, a letter?" she said, voice muffled by her arms.

"You can write to him and tell him anything you want to share, even how much you miss him. There's no right way to do it—you can write whatever you want, as much or as little as you feel like."

She lifted her head. "Can I listen to music?" she said.

I nodded.

"Okay."

An hour later, as the ninety-minute class period was ending, she asked me to print out the letter. The bell indicating the start of the lunch period played over the loudspeaker, but she stayed. "Will you read it?" she asked.

A Letter to Papa

Papa it's really bout to be a year that he took you from me papa ion know if i'm going to be good. He took you from me on 4/28 and all I was doing was cry, cry and cry but now it's hard for me not to cry it's not fair to me. How most people still have they papa and my papa was taking from me for nothing? Papa I had a lot to tell you but now I can't tell you nothing papa. I just want you back sometimes I be like why can't I have my papa just why. Papa you was like my daddy. That was fucked up what that boy did to you but god going to hale him. We just have to wait on it but his time going to come. I just hate not having you here with me papa. But I can't keep letting this stop me from doing what I have to do to make you happy. Papa I was so, so, so, so hurt that day when I got that phone call from Anthony. My heart stop for a long time. I couldn't do nothing but cry and say why just why. You never did nothing to nobody but helped them and for him to do that was fucked up man. Papa I just want you back. I need you back. I know you my angel now n you looking over me. You in a better place now but i just need you. I miss everything about you. I miss your phone calls. I miss your smile. I miss when you used to come by the house. Just to come see us. I miss our lil talking. I just miss everything I wish we had more time together but god wanted you home man, but why it had to be so soon? I don't like putting R.I.P in front of your name at all, I don't like seeing you on t-shirts papa, I just can't stop thinking about you. What happened to you is the hardest thing, i'm never going to get pass it papa. I know you don't like me crying but I can't help but cry at times. Sometimes I just need to cry, I have to let it out. Papa, you will never be forgotten, you always going to be on my mind. Papa remember that day you called me and I was in class and just kept calling and calling until I answered the phone and I was like papa i'm in class and you was like, "Ohh I didn't know you was still in school." Then you ask me how I been. What I been doing and we had a long talk on the phone that day. Remember when you came got us and we went to the store and we was talking about the people that was in the store. Remember for my 15th birthday I want to be with you that whole day and I came by your house. I was so happy to be with you. We had soo much fun that day too. Papa remember when me Jelly Anthony and Mason came sleep by your house and we was sitting outside talking all night and grandma came outside and was like y'all need to come inside now. But we had plenty more memories and I wish we can have more. I love you so much and I'm really missing you like crazy papa.

The feelings she had expressed were so well-known to me, it almost hurt. I told her how beautiful the letter was and asked if she wanted a hug. She said yes, then left to get in line for pizza at the cafeteria. I closed the door to my now-empty classroom and what I thought about next was the conversation I'd had a few weeks earlier about cigarettes.

I'd told P that my sister had been a smoker—that on her very first visit to New Orleans she claimed the pack I found in her purse was for a friend. And that I, too, had been one for a week in Indonesia, where I smoked sweet cloves with cups of coffee. When P said, "Tell me more," I thought he was going add "about Emily." But he meant more about me. I shrugged and said, "There's not much more to tell." I wished he had asked about Emily, had invited me to share more memories, had given me a reason to bring her back to life as something more than an obstacle, something more than a journal entry, something more than sick, than dead, than one-dimensional, than transgressive, than a cause, than an expertise lent to conversations about *13 Reasons Why* because I am, after all, the person in the room who has some experience with suicide, some stake in how it's represented, some sensitivity to joke after joke after joke about killing oneself.

I walked over to my computer and typed my sister's name into Google. Just to remember, just to feel.

OVER THE SUMMER, P AND I took a trip to the beach with our families. We stayed at Bubbie's beach house with my mother, stepfather, Ches, and Bubbie; P's parents and youngest brother stayed at a hotel two blocks away. On the Fourth of July, P and I woke up early to run. A couple miles in, surrounded by dune grass, sand, and sea, P pulled a ring from the pocket of his running shorts and asked, "Will you marry me?" I said yes, and I felt happy. I loved P. I loved that he was willing to spend his life with me. In this, there was security. And a feeling that approximated balance too: three years and three months after Emily's death, I'd been given a reason to celebrate, rather than mourn, publicly.

When we got back to the house, we played a game: we didn't say anything. My family was still waking up, and P's family wasn't due to join us for another hour. When his parents and brother arrived, the nine of us sat around the house drinking coffee, eating hot old-fashioned doughnuts from a greasy white paper bag, and chatting casually. After an hour, I picked up a section from the newspaper, held it in front of my face, and waited for someone to notice the diamond. It took another ten minutes. Then a chorus of joyous shouts.

Once the ring on my finger was no longer a novelty, I began to feel dread. In my head, the event of my wedding would only serve to highlight the huge hole that Emily had left. There couldn't be a bridal party; there couldn't be speeches. I imagined myself standing in a white dress on the hypothetical happiest day of my life and thinking only of my sister's absence. I thought about the *Modern Love* essay "A Brother as Significant as Any Other"—the idea of the role of significant other filled by a sibling, and how maybe, if Emily had stuck around, that is the way we would have been. In which case I wouldn't need a romantic partner. I wouldn't have to get married at all.

I was relieved to have some space at the end of July when I left New Orleans to go to graduate school and P stayed behind. We swore we'd make long distance work, but the 881 miles between us cleaved us root to stem. Rather, I let myself be distracted, giving less and less, neglecting the relationship's needs and hastening its death. Toward the end, P wrote me to say he was running out of motivation to try to feel connected to me. After I read the message, I screamed in my car to a song turned all the way up. I scared myself with how long and loud it was—I hadn't known I had that much air, that much sound, that much confusion and anger and frustration and loneliness and pain inside of me. I became almost disoriented, detached, hearing myself yell with ears that weren't my own, eyes that weren't mine staring out of the window into a world that could have been anywhere.

I ended up calling off the engagement after less than four months. Looking back, the decision seems obvious, almost necessary, predetermined—like it was not even truly a choice. My journals from the years I spent with J and with P are filled with complaints: "I don't want to be in a relationship," "I just want to be on my own." Yet it was terrifying to let go of a love that seemed certain. To release back into the wild a whole life I could have had, without quite knowing what it was I was looking for.

PART 4

WHEN I BEGAN GRADUATE SCHOOL, I was twenty-seven and on my own for the first time in five years. Outside of taking classes and teaching undergraduates and babysitting to supplement my income as a teaching assistant, I was languishing. Calls and texts went unanswered; the only thing I cooked, if it counts, was coffee. I managed to turn tasks that might have taken two hours into tasks that took two weeks. I could not sit still, or else all I could do was sit.

In the midst of this, I fell into an intense, brief friendship with a student in my program who often walked around barefoot on campus. We'd bonded when I'd recognized the tattoo on the top of his foot as the "falling man"—a symbol used by the band Third Eye Blind (who adopted the image from the death tarot card created by Salvador Dalí). On Sundays I went to his house and cuddled up beside his gray pit bull while he yelled enthusiastic obscenities at football games on TV. This reminded me of my father, who celebrated each first down made by the Giants and cursed at the referees. My new friend was smart and brazen and sharp-witted and thoughtful and fun and made me feel cared for, understood. I took comfort in his presence. He also disquieted me.

He'd been having a hard time, struggling to manage his mental health and to cope with his cousin's fatal overdose. He meant it when he said, "It should've been me instead."

I described to him the nothingness of my existence in the year after Emily died. How pointless it felt to be alive until I stood at the top of the Kepler Track in New Zealand in the misty purple-gray morning light, breathing thin air, a speck in a red knit cap among the snowcapped tops of mountains, and finally, finally felt that perhaps it might be possible to live without my sister. I told him not to give up.

But not giving up does exactly nothing. It doesn't magically erase diagnosed mental illness or excise one's wish to be dead. One moment my friend would be sitting at a white plastic table outside the school gym eating a slice of pizza and the next he'd disappear into the dark woods and return swollen-faced, dripping blood. I wanted to hold him. I wanted to throw up. I wanted to fill the Emily-shaped void in my body. I wanted it all to stop.

I began to dress things in tahini and soy sauce, in candle wax, too, and sometimes weed and sometimes wine. I sat on the carpeted floor of my new bedroom and did not know where I was: white noise would blow and geese would race across the pond outside my window and I'd sit there all cotton, all crumpled and soft. I tried to embrace it, the discomfort. I thought of how simple it was to be alone when I closed my curtains so neighbors couldn't see—no one was looking, but I wanted to be sure. (Other times, I walked around naked, forgot they were there.) I told myself it was okay; I did not need to be seen. It was not sad to be alone—to inhabit a space that left room for distraction, for molasses, spun sugar being stretched. Swallowing itself, so thin in the middle it looked like it was breaking. I checked myself for cracks, for signs of decay—what I wanted to see was red. Wanted to see vessels torn open, skin pulled away in strings. I wanted to see how deep my pain went, where it ended, what it was siphoning from me. I would have given it away if I could've. Would have washed it in lavender soap and let it dry in the sun as the breeze dropped and then folded it, one tidy thing in the middle of a war.

MY FATHER AND STEPMOTHER DROVE down to North Carolina to see me toward the end of September. Nana, too, but she couldn't handle such a long drive with her bad back, so she flew. The first night of their visit, they took me out to eat at a seafood restaurant that my father chose based on online reviews. We were by the ocean, after all. We sat in a wooden booth beneath a fake straw-thatched roof, surrounded by plastic tropical plants and primary colors, a seaweed-draped mermaid painted on the wall.

Our meal was a continual circle, a passing of food from plate to plate, the typical monitoring of what everyone else ate. After appetizers of cold shrimp and squishy crab cakes and clam chowder, I began to stack our empty bowls and small plates. My stepmother passed two dishes to me.

My father burped. "Excuse me."

"Little you!" I singsonged. Childlike was my default mode in my father's company—both to draw out his own goofiness and to preempt tension, keep the mood as light as it could be.

"It's been a long time since I've heard that!" my father exclaimed.

"What?" said Nana.

"We used to—that was a little expression among our family," he said.

"Big me, little me, medium me," I explained.

"That I never heard," Nana said.

"You must not have been listening—we said it all the time!" I teased. I then took a deep breath and advantage of the good mood. "Hey, at some point, while you're here, can I ask you guys some questions? About Emily? For some writing I'm trying to work on?"

There was a stillness. I pressed my thumb into the saltine cracker crumbs on my paper placemat.

My stepmother spoke first. "Of course, sweet pea."

"Sure," said my father. "Whatever you need."

I felt Nana nod yes next to me.

On the morning they left, we sat outside at a café by my campus and ate breakfast: egg sandwiches on rye, hold the cheese, home fries with onions, well-done. I was running out of time to ask them to talk to me about Emily, but I was nervous to bring up the subject. It was hard to believe that in three and a half years we hadn't talked about her beyond what had been said in passing. Halfway through the meal, I said, "So, I still want to ask you about Emily. What do you remember?"

My father's response was to ask for a more specific question, but I didn't have any prepared.

"What's your goal for this conversation?" he asked.

"No goal. Just to have it."

The only sound was the crunch of teeth into toast.

"Um . . . just a memory. First memory that comes to mind."

Immediately, my stepmother responded, "Emily in the basement painting, and getting covered from head to toe while she was working on her projects. She took an old window shade and she painted on that. I believe we still have it—"

Nana interrupted. "Do you want a little bacon or no?"

"How old do you think she was?"

"About the same time she started playing trumpet. I remember she was practicing a lot and wasn't very good yet!" My stepmother chuckled.

"So, she was probably nine or ten," I said. We'd both started learning to play our instruments through our school district's band program in fourth grade.

"What comes to me all the time," said Nana, smiling, "is every time I wanted to take a picture of her, she would stick out her tongue or make a funny face. But then when she came to visit one summer, she promised me that I could take a picture of her, or that she'd take a picture for me. And then she took a picture of her eye. Just her eye!" Nana laughed. "And I used to like to cook with her."

"What'd you cook?"

"We'd start out with one thing, and then it became a mishmash! But mostly, she liked to make, uh, cookies. And cakes. And she would say, 'The other things, Nana, you can make for me, instead of showing me how to make it.' We cut up fruit together—lots of fruit. Lots and lots of fruit."

Nana paused. Fork tines tapped plates. "I'm trying to think. I remember her talking, and she loved the farm in Maine, and she loved the cat there. She showed me pictures of it. And she said she liked to go in the fields and see the bugs and the butterflies. So those are the things she really loved, the things of nature. And the last time I had seen her—no, it was on the phone, we talked. And she said that she would love to have a farm and grow all-natural vegetables and fruits and everything and have—"

"As opposed to the unnatural ones," my father teased.

She continued, "People who have eating disorders come. And she had thought of a role that everyone from our family would have—your uncle, your cousins, cooking, helping in the garden."

"Yeah, I remember that," I said. "Do you remember when her eating disorder was really bad? Do any of you have memories of that time?"

My father and grandmother immediately said, "Yes."

Nana described taking Emily shopping and how she wouldn't get a blouse because she said she looked fat in it. Then added, "But you know what I remember the most? When she was in a play. And I can shut my eyes now and picture her with the makeup, and dancing around—that was Emily!"

"It brings up a lot of painful, unresolved things for me," said my father. He sat beside me, his voice a quiet quiver. "Because—it doesn't feel comfortable, me talking to you about this, because a lot of things were done wrong, in my opinion. And there's nothing to be done about it now. It's only going to, you know, create more tension and stress. I'm not sure I want to do that to you."

"Well . . ." I hesitated. "Yeah. I hear you. I'm curious to know, though."

My father recounted everything then with a failed urgency: how Emily stole $300 in cash from him and "I blew up at her and she got all upset" and she called our mom and our mom came to pick her up and he was sure then (though he was speculating) that our mother commiserated with Emily and "talked about all of the terrible things or scary things that I did or whatever" and this was the start of the cold silence between them that lasted for four years, because my mother switched Emily to a different therapist whose idea it was that he wasn't to have any contact with Emily until she was "over things."

It was clear to him, he continued, that our mother had "brainwashed" us. (Instead of considering I might be expressing my own feelings in my childhood journal, he assumed that the words "I wish Dad was dead" that I'd written across the page in big letters were something I'd overheard my mother say about him.) He said she wanted him out of the picture altogether, and that she used this incident between him and Emily as a way to shut him out, though he was "probably the strongest source of love! and security!"—these words emphasized by a hand to the table—"in her life! Things could have been much different, and they weren't."

Nana had begun to cry. "Becca, I just want that—the two of you—we've had such a good time together this weekend. I don't want it to end on a negative note, now that Dad's bringing up things that would hurt you. It has to be very hard for you, hearing these things."

"I'm not—I'm okay," I said firmly. And I was. None of this felt new to me. None of this felt shocking. I didn't say what I was thinking—that I couldn't imagine any tension or stress between my father and me greater than that which I long ago learned to endure.

My father continued, "After Emily passed, I said to myself, 'Why would I want to make this any worse than it already is?' So, I've kept all this stuff inside so that no one else has to suffer anymore." His voice grew quieter. "But when we talk about, you know—it just inherently brings all that up."

Nana steered the conversation back to Emily, recalling how Emily had said something about wishing she could get off her drugs, about not wanting to take them forever, and that she wanted to drop out of school and work on the farm.

My stepmother confirmed, "She said the same thing to me, about the farm, but your mother wouldn't let her."

The waitress came to check on us and clear our plates. Cars drove past and birds chirped and trilled from perches on power lines and trees.

"What else?" I asked.

"Lots of stuff, I don't know," said my father. But the hurt had left his voice.

"You can tell me! It's okay. I'm okay. I'm grateful that you guys are sharing with me. I haven't asked you before and that's why I'm asking now."

"Yeah, I mean, all the good memories go back to pre–eating disorder stuff," said my father. "For the most part."

"Well, it doesn't just have to be good memories. What's coming to mind?"

There was a long pause. Across from me, Nana chimed in, "Emily had come to visit me, and when she left, my scale was gone. And she also took a skirt."

I squeezed out a hollow laugh. "That is, unfortunately, not shocking."

My grandmother then took my hand into hers and, in a soft voice, asked, "Can I ask a question? I was never told. There were a lot of things that your father kept from me. And you were upset, and I didn't want to ask any questions. But I want to know so that I can have a little closure."

"Of course."

"How did Emily die? No one ever told me."

My breath caught in my chest. How had nobody told her? I knew how exhausting it was to wonder. She'd held on to that question, that tiny and giant and terrible question, for three and a half years.

On Monday, Emily goes to class like she's supposed to and then on Tuesday she just stays in bed. Doesn't put anything in order—sits around and waits until most of the campus is most likely to be asleep, unaware. Places an order online for one last dinner to be delivered. Doesn't watch movies to pass the time—stares into space. When it is finally late enough—early enough the next morning—she goes to the bathroom and gets dressed. Jeans and an old T-shirt. Puts on a coat and grabs her keys. Her hands shake. She walks down a

flight of stairs and goes outside. The stars. The air. She lights
a cigarette. The weather is cold and fair. Her green car is
parked down the block. She pulls it around to the front of
the residence hall and puts it in park. Goes back upstairs to
her room, gets the cardboard box and a bucket, carries it all
downstairs. Tears the box into pieces and uses them to cover
the car windows so no one will see a dead body first thing
in the morning on their way to class. Duct tape to cover the
air vents. A note in the window with a warning: be careful
of the gas. She closes the doors and mixes the chemicals
and gets into the driver's seat. Starts coughing. Buckles in
so she won't slump against the horn. Radio? Probably not.
Risk of being heard—she is careful not to make too much
noise. Doesn't feel herself inside her body—wants so badly to
pass out so she can stop wondering if it's going to work. She
drowns on land as her lungs fill with gas. It smells of rotten
eggs, this one last effort to get herself through the pain. She
knows: this too shall pass.

On Wednesday morning, around seven or eight, a few
adults stand around the car in disbelief—not quite right,
something strange, something off. Shock. A phone call, 911,
ambulance, police car, fire truck. The school is small; rumors
spread fast. After twenty-one years, one month, and less than
a day, she died. Perhaps it is true that some people are not
meant to stay in the world very long—it would keep things
nice and neat.

I TOOK A WEEKEND TRIP to Colorado that November to visit my stepfamily—my grandparents and aunt and uncle and cousins, the ones who'd kept Emily safe for the weeks that she was still severely depressed after inpatient treatment had ended. During the visit, I went on walks along a creek and counted turtles, attended a Catholic high school's production of *Fiddler on the Roof*, and ate and threw up and slept.

On the morning I left, I stared out the car window, watching the undertones of the clouds change from golden to purple against the snowcapped mountains. One cloud was so thick and wide it stunned a whole low swath of sky, turning it a muted shade of indigo-gray. How wide things are out West—how open. As she drove me to the airport, my aunt told me to stay open. Spoke of plans and how life dodges, diverts, redirects them. Said, "Emily's death was a wrecking ball—it tore through your life, our whole family." Said there might still be a chance to get back together with P. Said, "I just want someone to wrap you up in love. Life is meant to be shared."

As I waited in the security line, I scanned faces: older couples with frail bones, men whose eyes held no particular warmth or kindness. I felt lost in a future hopelessness, a future frustration, a future regret—was not yet convinced that I hadn't made a mistake in breaking off my engagement to P. The feeling was a sinking. In the car, I'd heard myself laugh and it was so obvious to me that an alien had been moving my limbs, pumping my blood, taking my toothbrush and sticking it down my throat. My eyes watered as I stood and stared. *Life is meant to be shared.*

I'd been trying to share, but I couldn't seem to figure out how to do it. When I'd gotten engaged, I'd felt happy, then felt nothing. Felt nothing, no one, could be so sure as to spend a whole life together. I wondered what else would go wrong, how my heart would break, how I would survive it. I couldn't comprehend how they'd done it twice, my mom and her mom. It seemed better to stick to loving small: to watch the sky and clouds, etchings of rain, birdsong in the air, the warm smell of grass, the way the dark can turn a whisper to a shout. The clinging of sunshine to skin, how light gathers, how glow radiates. Clean and simple. Safe and small.

I was on a plane again two weeks later, this time to Philadelphia. Before I spent Thanksgiving, as usual, with my father's extended family, I stayed for a night at my mother's. As dinner was wrapping up, I wandered away from the table, at first to deposit all of my food into the toilet and then to be with the things in my sister's room. I don't know how long I was gone—long enough that Ches was sent upstairs to retrieve me for dessert and found me in Emily's secret closet, the one whose entrance is disguised by the thick dark cork that panels the surrounding wall, the one that holds the relics of her Jewish education, as if she meant to establish in that small, dark space a secret altar. There were silver candlesticks patterned with cutouts of stars, white candles still in them, given to her on her bat mitzvah, during which she gave an impassioned speech. There were two books of prayer, *siddurim*—the plural for *siddur,* a word that comes from the Hebrew root *sdr,* which means "order," which is related both to ritual and control—to organizing the universe and giving meaning to things.

And so maybe that is what religion does or what it is meant to do, and maybe that is what I am trying to do here: maybe all of my writing is only a prayer, a plea, a search for order, a neurotic need to assign meaning to things. One of the prayer books is white and one has a blue fabric cover on it that our mother decorated. I have them, too, though my thin fabric cover is tan and depicts a dove because my Hebrew name is Tziporah, which means "bird." Hers has on it a tree, the Tree of Life, because her Hebrew name is Chaya, which means "alive, living." These are things she is no longer, but perhaps that was the hope for her. It is possible that on some cellular level our parents knew that for her to live would be a struggle, and so the name became an asking, a begging to the gods or god to let this girl live.

How hard it must be to be a parent. They blame themselves, I think—it burns through their skin like menthol, lingering mercilessly. To lose a sibling is awful; to lose a child disrupts the natural order of things. And yet I, too, took care of her. I know it's not the same. But I tried to keep her safe.

I returned to an empty apartment in North Carolina—both of my roommates were still away for the holiday. I sat on the black faux leather couch in the living room with my feet tucked beneath me, a stack of student papers on my lap, and flipped to a football game on TV. Instead of grading poems, I let myself be distracted by the roaring crowd. As the camera panned to the benches, I thought about what it's like to sit on the sidelines, helpless as you watch your team lose. What builds inside of you when you don't have the chance to step up, step in, step on the field to do what you can in the way you know how. To spectate is a kind of imagining: think of all that difference you could make. To play is to know just how much is not within your control; it is to know that you are never really enough and that the ball slipped through your hands because you couldn't help but close your eyes. There is so much fault, and it burns and burns. Afterward all you can do is wake up each day and take it, knowing all you have done is all you can do. Such knowledge is maddening. Like water poured over sand, it dampens, dissolves, disappears.

CHES WAS ACCEPTED TO COLLEGE while I was back in Delaware during winter break, and my grand idea was ice cream. So we stood, my mother and I, clutching three cold cartons of Ben & Jerry's in the Wawa checkout line.

The cigarettes were waiting there, above the cashier's head, tucked into their lofted beds. I joked that we should get a pack—I didn't smoke more than "not very often." My mother's eyes sparked for a second. She told me to choose, and I pointed at the American Spirits, the ones that my friends who were cool smoked in college. She asked for the blue pack.

"This is what I do with my friend. We buy a pack and smoke one in the parking lot. Then we leave the pack for someone else to find. Otherwise, I'd smoke them all," she told me.

My mother and I smoked outside the convenience store, standing in the dark winter night, in between empty parking spaces. Another mother had taken her here once, after Emily died. They'd just stood, middle-aged, smoking cigarettes. She'd said to my mother, "Anytime you want to meet and smoke in the parking lot, let me know." I nodded along. What a nice gesture that was.

And then it spilled out, the whole story: how the blue pack came to my mother from the funeral home nearly four years ago, alongside the change in the pockets of the clothes that had clung to Emily's body, also blue.

I asked my mother if she still had them. I asked if she ever smoked them.

"No, because they have that poison."

I thought maybe she meant the slow poison, the carcinogens, that all cigarettes have. Then I realized she meant the lime sulfur that my sister used to poison herself, the twenty bottles of it. I hadn't quite gotten that. Is that a thing that one is supposed to quite get?

She said she still had it all—I imagined a thick wad of material, a bundle of cotton and Lycra, copper pennies and denim, tar and tobacco. I was curious about where she kept it. But I didn't ask, and she didn't tell me. She said, tears welling, "I just can't." Can't go there, to a place that is hidden—a place I won't look for, I promised. A place that neither my stepfather nor half sibling knows. I was not even sure she herself knew where it was. Maybe it is better that way. Maybe some days she wakes and thinks it was all a dream: that displacement, that dissonance, that uncertainty of the site of anything.

Later that week, I walked into my mother's room as she was folding T-shirts into thirds and pairing socks. I sat down on her bed beside the piles of clothes and began to fidget with my necklace. I had come to inform her of my intention to go through Emily's things. I didn't want to have a discussion. If I asked for permission, she might deny me access; without permission, she might find my presence in Emily's room suspect.

"I guess I don't really understand what you want to do with all that stuff," she said in response. "Are you looking for answers?"

"No!" I snapped. What I'd heard in the question was my mother's distrust and the insinuation of my own desperation.

"It's a fair question!"

"No! I don't have a plan, I don't have an itinerary. I'm just trying to see what—it's not about looking for answers. I'm trying to write, but I don't know what shape it is or even what it is yet, and I'm trying to figure it out. I don't know how else to explain it. I don't know if I can put it in more concrete terms. I don't know what I'm looking for. So, I'm trying to look at everything. And then I'm going to see how it comes together. It's not like I'm writing a memoir to blame people for things. Or giving a minute by minute account. It's more like . . . I don't know exactly. But that's why I need you to trust me. And I don't know how else to establish that except to ask you to trust me."

"Can you look at me for a second?" she said. I'd long ago developed a habit of avoiding eye contact while speaking, afraid that if I glimpsed judgment, I'd lose my nerve or train of thought; my gaze was fixed on the green plastic square of laundry basket beside my mother.

I shifted my focus; her eyes were watering.

"It's not about trusting you. It's about giving away what I have left of her. I can't have you taking her things without us talking about it. There are things of hers that I have not been able to go through yet." Her voice was gentle and a little sad.

"I'm not trying to keep anything—I just want to share," I said.

"I'm happy to share with you," she said. "Actually, I'm not happy. I'm scared to lose control over what I have of her. Okay? And some of that stuff needs to go in the trash. I know that. I'm not there yet. It's not about not trusting you with her things, her physical things. You want to come and spend ten hours in her room? Be my guest. You want to go through all that shit? Be my guest. But don't take things until we talk about it. Okay?"

I nodded yes.

Because I'd lost Emily's laptop three years earlier (I truly
don't know what happened to it: I might have misplaced it, it
might have been stolen—it seemed to just disappear), her red
external hard drive was my only means of access to the files
on her computer. But my mother said it wasn't working. My
stepfather had taken it to Best Buy, where the Geek Squad
said they were unable to fix it.

I sat on the floor of my bedroom, connected the external
hard drive to my own laptop, and messed with it until, eventually, I got it working. Then I began to look through the photos
and home videos Emily had squirrelled away: me, Emily, and
Ches lying together in a hammock, all in fall sweaters, gri-
macing at the camera as we're told, "Please just pose for one
presentable photo while Becca is home for Thanksgiving";
the three of us dressed up and holding hands as we dance
together in the hotel ballroom where my college hosted a
commencement party; my hands on Emily's cheeks, forcing
her face into a smile at Ches's b'nai mitzvah party.

I shared the pictures on social media, compelled by—
what? Something about connection, about being seen, about
intersubjectivity. Only after several friends sent me messages
containing little red hearts did I experience emotion; imagining them imagining me feeling sad or wistful or lonely allowed
me to acknowledge that I might actually be.

The next day, I discovered that I was able to access
Emily's old email accounts. It hadn't occurred to me to try
before, but it turned out to be relatively easy: I knew the
answers to all the security questions, the names of her childhood best friend and oldest cousin and the make and model
of her first car (it was mine before it was hers).

There were over 9,999 unread messages in her inbox—
all junk. I searched for "Becca" and also "sister," but there
was no trace of me. All I wanted was to have been there. I

felt a compulsion to delete all the unread messages—to orga-
nize, clean, and clear. I don't know why. Maybe I was trying
to peel back further the layers of her existence, to get closer
to some answer or truth. I began to delete.

When I came across the subject line "Do You Love Your
Mother?" I clicked on it. Marketing for Mother's Day gifts.
But the question made me think. Not about whether I loved
my mother, but what I could learn to accept and/or live with.

The night before, I'd gone up to Philly with my mother
and stepfather. The sky was a fiery mix of light, a backdrop
to flocks of birds diving like fighter kites. We had gone to a
film at the Ritz Five theater. On the bathroom mirror was a
laminated sign:

THIS HAND DRYER IS MOTION ACTIVATED. PLEASE
DO NOT PLACE YOUR POPCORN UNDER THE SENSOR.

Afterward, we discussed the film over bitter hot tea and
steamed green dumplings and salty yellow broth and the
bright red skin of roasted pork. The meal had been pleas-
ant enough. Then the subject switched, abruptly, to Emily.
My mother's question was reasonable—"Were you able to
recover Emily's music from her external hard drive?"—but it
sucked the color out of everything. Why couldn't we simply
sit at a restaurant in Chinatown that we'd been going to all
my life and discuss a movie? Why couldn't we talk about
me? Why was I still an intermediary?

I clicked on the trash can icon and deleted the Mother's
Day email, then continued to work my way through Emily's
inbox, scrolling through and through, tracing my fingertips
along the endless walls of an imaginary room. What was I
missing among bytes of information, in between subject lines?
The letters collected no dust, had no texture. No strange,

sweet taste on my tongue. If I needed a sample of her DNA, where would I find it? Would it have been better or worse if she'd left a note or some other lukewarm clue? I eventually noticed the time—I had been kneeling on the rug in my bedroom for three hours. There was nothing to unearth. My knees hurt, and I googled what it means to kneel: "a sign of reverence, submissiveness, deference—and sometimes mourning and vulnerability." I stretched across all of these things.

BACK AT SCHOOL, I BUMPED INTO A PROFESSOR as I wandered through the hallways of the creative writing department. It was Valentine's Day. She was getting ready to teach, and I was dressed for a run, procrastinating—avoiding both my work and the cold. We chatted for a minute near a corkboard covered in flyers for writing contests and events on campus. The professor told me her teenage daughter had recently written an essay titled "Running Is My Boyfriend." We smiled.

"She's got her priorities straight."

I said goodbye, walked outside, started my watch, and began my run: six miles along a wooded path. The afternoon was sunny and the pace was fast, speed fueled by uncertainty, clouds in contrast moving past. The wind blanketed everything, tasted like every man I'd ever tried to love. I was alone, and wasn't this what I wanted?

Suddenly, it hurt to breathe—I felt sharp iron slicing through my back, my side, my brain. I had a heavy hunch that I had done something wrong in life, in love. It wasn't clear to me whether my choice to be alone was steadying or a wild thing, a bucking bull waiting to toss me off its back. I felt unsettled, suspended in a pond made of mud, unsure if it would ever come to an end, the seeking. Nothing and everything moved too slowly. I felt myself a burden, the whole weight of me: ups and downs of moods and energy. The illusion I gave of being open, the quick need to shut down again. My impulse to hold on to closeness, entwined with the knowledge of loss that had needled itself into my bones. What would it be like just to be? To let go of the need to make sense of each thing that will disappear.

Nearly two weeks later, my roommate came home from his job at an elementary school with a big bag of animal crackers. It was Emily's twenty-fifth birthday, and right away I recalled how in college, after hours, we used to take the Writing Center keys (which we had access to as employees) and unlock the cabinet full of ceramic mugs, bags of tea, and a giant plastic tub of animal crackers: late-night sustenance in the library. We'd grab handfuls of the cookies and microwave water, then sit in fat blue armchairs across from a wall of windows that reflected the night's darkness and blurred together our bodies. Corners of chins and sharp knees, dipping elephant trunks into mugs of mint tea.

From the December before she died:

hey

just so you know

i think you're soooo great

hey now! i think you're so great. i really really do

and i'm sitting in the writing center working

staring at the animal crackers and wishing i could give you some

GUESS WHAT

there were animal crackers at my planning period
faculty meeting!

and i took like 2 cupfuls haha

so you should eat some with me

hahaha maybe i will in your honor

haha perfect

how are you today?

i'm ok. anxious and wanting to be in bed mostly. hah

i'm sorry dude

meds not helping?

i'm in that weird transition phase where i'm increased to a higher dose of the mood stabilizer, but no—not really right now

yeah yeah

i gotchya

you're being really patient

you kow

hahah

you KOX

oops

COW

COCKS

hahahaha

whaaaat

OVER MEMORIAL DAY WEEKEND, I traveled north. On the evening I arrived, I went first to my father and stepmother's house to join them for dinner: a huge green salad my step-mom put together, lemonade from scratch in a quart-sized deli container, and the little disks of fried salmon croquettes that were one of my father's specialties.

Once we'd eaten, my father and I went to the basement to play Ping-Pong. Surrounded by empty cardboard boxes and dust-covered stacks of craft kits, puzzles, and toys from my childhood, we hit the little white ball back and forth. I asked him to tell me more about him and my mother. I learned that they met at a dance when they were freshmen, and that I wasn't planned but Emily was. "Look how well that turned out!" my father joked.

In the morning, I met up with Emily's ex-girlfriend at the same coffee shop in Delaware where she used to work and where Emily used to go to do homework or study. Always prepared to befriend and/or charm somebody, my sister would strike up a conversation each time she ordered a dirty chai latte. I'd never gotten to know Emily's girlfriend during the years they were together—I had been skeptical because she was five years older than Emily, who was just barely eighteen when they began dating. She loved my sister, though. I know because as we talked, she told me she recognized what's shared between us, the things I often forget are still there: my voice, my laugh, certain gestures and faces I make. The time I spent with her forced me to think about what it means to still exist as Emily's sister: how I might bring a person closer to Emily, unwittingly; how I can only ever know myself as myself and so, for me, she will still not be there.

After coffee, I went to my mother's house. No one was there, and the solitude made it feel safe to go into Emily's room. It was what I liked about going home. There was nowhere else I could randomly soak her in, touch her things. I tried on the clothes I thought might fit me, then wandered into the attic, lifted the lids of large storage bins. I sat in a skirt of Emily's, sweating in the stale heat, and read through a million old letters that she'd saved. And our dead aunt's journal, which I found tucked beneath newborn pajamas, a blank-faced doll, Emily's favorite Tigger T-shirt, a hand-knit sweater, our parents' wedding album. The journal was a spiral-bound notebook, three sections with fifty sheets each, college ruled. Her blue-ink letters looped through a mind drowning itself in doubt and monotony—the stuckness of depression. Thirty-one years before my sister died, my aunt Stephanie wrote:

> **January 26.** What can I do? I can do nothing about nothing for nothing. I feel like dying. I won't do any-thing to myself because it won't work. It never does. I'll just end up owing money to hospitals. Money I don't have. It's better if I don't have a job because then I don't see what I'm missing. Like being happy and going out and doing things. Why should I bother to be happy and try & fight this depression? So I can get well to get sick again? I know I'm going to be sick for the rest of my life.

It's inevitable. When I said that to Dr. V he told me not to worry about it. He said concentrate on getting well. Why? So I can get sick again? I hate life. Dr. V can't help me. I've talked to fucking psychiatrists my whole life and I'm still sick. No one can help me. I want to die. I never feel like getting up in the morning. Why? I never enjoy myself. I hate myself. I hate myself I hate myself. I will never be happy again. I *hate* myself!!! I wish I were dead. I have nothing to live for. I try to talk to Mom but she doesn't understand. Nobody does.

March 26. Yesterday I went to the railroad tracks to lie in front of a train but when it came I couldn't stay there. Today I feel better.

It struck me that during one of her lower points, the entries could have been written by Emily. I wondered if it was helpful that my mother had this person as an older sister, if it prepared her for Emily's illness or taught her how to take care of someone so sick.

I found Emily's poetry notebook, too, in the attic—a middle school project I didn't know existed. She'd clearly taken the assignment seriously. The dedication to Mom and me—"Both of whom are *the only* two people who have been there all my life. Their support has been *unconditionally* given to me, whether I was in a state to return it or not."—and her use of emphasis like a melodramatic middle finger to her imagined reader. The Dickinson poems about death and grief, which meant something different to her then, than they do, thanks to her, now to me. And the last page. A photo of her face, age three, missing one front tooth, so smiley, brown curls abounding, and Thoreau's words above it. Was it only ever always a matter of time?

That afternoon, my stepfather drove my mother, Ches, and me to Harpers Ferry, West Virginia, where ten members of my extended family had gathered in a rented house on top of a grassy hill to celebrate Bubbie's eightieth birthday. Upon arrival, I took up the task of unpacking. This mainly involved an improbable number of bags of groceries, and I began by doing the thing I always do when I am with my family and feeling anxious: I rearranged the refrigerator. I surveyed its contents, shuffling sticks of butter in wax paper and bottles of old ketchup, clearing a shelf for salad dressing and filling a clear drawer with different cheeses. It was a game of Tetris—trying to put things in order, to make everything fit.

My mother saw me doing this and heard the shortness with which I responded to my great aunt when she asked me a question about diet soda—the clipped tone that means something is bothering me. She said, "Oh stop—just go for a run."

I got up, put on my sneakers, and stormed out of the house. To run was default—a way to simultaneously process my feelings and escape them. The run was slow and the sun was setting. Small yellow pine warblers flew alongside a zip-zagging split rail fence, and toads croaked their presence from tall grasses. My anger slipped off into a hole somewhere in the ground and, in its place, a new calm rested in me.

I SPENT THE REMAINDER OF THAT SUMMER in North Carolina, running, babysitting, and reading through old letters and journals. Every day it was exhausting. Every day it hurt to see who I used to be, what has always preoccupied me. I cringed at my youth, my naivety—those skins I thought I'd shed as I'd grown. The truth was that they were still there, old thoughts like stretch marks, unfading.

At night, sleep eluded me. There was a fear, an emptiness, like nothing could contain me. All I could see was what was missing. Like the little metal heart-shaped earring I'd found at the bottom of a blue bag in my closet: in my mind it was Emily's, though it almost couldn't be. At what point do I give up the possibility that there are pieces of her in the places she used to be? If I wanted to, I could find a way to turn her into anything, could make her everywhere.

When I'd daydreamed about going back to school to write, I had no sense of how draining this book would be—how much it would hurt to keep prying at the knots of a tight, tangled line of time, emotion, memory. I wished I could stop, wished I'd never started writing at all. I didn't know how to connect the dots—didn't know what order. There is no order. There are moments, there are memories, there are spaces in between. It didn't make sense. It doesn't still. The story circled in on itself as soon as it started: a spiral seeping through my skull, turning gusts of wind into sand into ghosts. I felt desperate to be free of the dense, sticky pool of grief's pull—how it consumed me. And yet, I'd chosen this—

No, I hadn't. Not my sister dying, not my mind's wanderings, not my family. Should it have always been obvious? Was it clear to everyone except me? It doesn't matter how many months it has been, how far removed I am from that phone call. I am forever tied to time; it's all that links me to her. Even though it shrinks and stretches, even though I've untangled small strands of it nice and neat, this will never be over. How naive I had been to believe time might mean something, to believe enough time might mean something different is possible for me.

I want her to know that it matters, her leaving. I want her to know that I love her and the missing hurts. It's a sprinkler going off just after a storm's ended—a spot of mud that just sits in the shade, just stays. How else to explain the feeling of being lost and okay simultaneously? She was in so much pain and I have no one to blame: not myself, not our parents, not my sister or her doctors or the medicine or Big Pharma, not her assailant, not our college, not our genes.

AT THE END OF AUGUST, I visited my stepfamily in Colorado. One afternoon, my aunt covered her kitchen island counter with red-and-white-striped dish towels, upon which she laid an army of quilted crystal canning jars, their metal bands and lids, a pair of tongs, a wooden spoon, two plastic wide-mouthed funnels, and a cardboard box containing half a bushel of Palisade peaches. I washed my hands beneath a window, then donned an apron and set to work beside my aunt and twelve-year-old cousin. The sounds were roiling water, the hiss of gas-fed flame; outside, the day was bright. While we sterilized the jars, the round, fleshy fruits basked patiently in sunlight. Once the peaches were blanched, their skins split beneath my thumbs and slipped right off, revealing the soft gold flesh that we quartered, sugared, boiled, and stirred continuously.

After all of the jars were filled with gooey amber and sealed finger-tight, my aunt, still wearing a pink Minnie Mouse apron, sat down on a stool, and I stood on the other side of the granite-topped counter, sipping water. My aunt said that if Emily were with us preserving peaches, she would be so sorry. I believed her—I agreed. On so many nights when Emily was alive she wanted to die; it was our job to help her keep herself here. The desire was a disease, a tumor, a cell that mutated and multiplied. It grew alongside her and attached itself to the person she meant to be—an undercurrent, malignant.

My aunt then asked what I thought my life might be like if my sister were still living, and I answered honestly: it would be so different. I never would have left the path, that old cliché—in a letter Emily wrote (not to me), she said that I'd followed it "probably unconsciously, very methodically." I'd done all the right things "on the surface, according to plan." And though I'd just finished college when she'd written the letter, and though she was younger than me, she knew I still had "so much more life to figure out. Not that we ever really figure it out anyway."

So yes—things would be different. I might have remained set in my ways and settled, settling. My decisions would revolve, as they did before, around Emily—everything, anything, to make sure she's okay. I wouldn't have the lack of obligation or the courage I gained when left in her wake—things that predicate wandering, deviation.

Is this the part, then, where I thank my sister for dying? Thank you for how you've released your monopoly on our attention, for the space you've given us to focus on other things: our health instead of yours, our own feelings. Thank you because our parents are so much better than I've ever known them to be: kinder, gentler, more generous and patient—almost even-keeled, self-aware. And other members of our family, and your friends, and mine: we're all still here, ongoing. In this, there is beauty: you are no longer defining. You are held in place—the missing is a hurt, not a pining. Without you, everything is motion and stillness, symmetry and distance, changed and unchanged simultaneously.

MY FAVORITE PLACE TO RUN in North Carolina was a four-mile loop around an L-shaped lake with fingers, fringed by pine trees and cypress knobs and great blue herons and geese that flap their wings against the water like they're clapping. I was there on a warm, clear day in September when I got the news that a hurricane was approaching. Residents were advised to evacuate.

I packed my car with clothes and books and a half-empty carton of oat milk from the fridge and cold brew coffee and my only plant, got on I-95 North, queued up the audiobook version of *A Little Life*, and made my way toward my mother's house.

During my displacement, I hopped from Delaware to Baltimore to Chicago to Boston, staying with a different friend in each city. I tried to stay cheerful, but I couldn't escape the anxiety: first of having no idea what would happen to the town and the people who couldn't leave, then of having no idea when I'd be able to return. I'd often excuse myself to the bathroom to check the latest weather forecast or local news headlines on my phone. The toilet paper was useful for blotting tears.

When it was finally safe to go back, after three long weeks, I got back on I-95, this time southbound, still working my way through *A Little Life*. When I got to the part in the book about Jude's grief, JB's retrospective exhibit, it hit me so hard I almost couldn't see the passing road or cars or trees: for the past four and a half years, what I had been looking for was evidence that my sister loved me. Words were not enough; to know, I needed the way she looked at me, understood me, brought me back to myself—the way she knew me.

I wanted to be known again—to have a person who would reflect myself back to me. I wanted something quiet, something simple, something that asked for little and yet still wanted to stay with me. I wanted the impossible, always: telepathy and heat lightning, cold ice in a glass that would melt into steam and slip along skin soundlessly. I wanted flesh. A thing to hold on to. Something separate from me. I wanted someone to bring me out of my head and into my body. I lose sight so easily, don't know what to think, am unsure of what is true. Is this a human thing? I am never sure when I will become too much to bear, when someone will have had enough of me. The only person with whom I did not experience this fear was Emily.

Within an hour of returning, I went back to the lake for a run. The water smelled like it had been held captive by a mad scientist. Trees lay dead asleep across sidewalks and lampposts were bent at angles associated with very broken arms. The flowers had forgotten they were not supposed to bloom in October—there were bits of pink and purple everywhere. After less than a slow, sorry mile I ended up walking—I couldn't make myself go through any other motion. I felt like a bit of a shell of a human. A bit floaty, bit unsure. I wanted to fast-forward, to outrun the loneliness. Instead, I got back in my car and stopped at a grocery store, filled my cart with cold currencies of sadness: ice cream, frozen cookie dough. What I really wanted was the connection, the togetherness that I was suddenly so acutely aware that I was missing.

I had tried to believe I didn't need my sister—it was just that the things I had of hers did not register as more than

shriveled facts. When I'd evacuated for the hurricane, I'd
left behind photos, postcards she'd written, a painting she
made for me. What was I thinking? Something about how
material objects don't matter, which I want to believe, but I
find myself caught in between, clinging to the plastic pepper
shaker of ashes that lives in a little black box beside my bed,
her books, her clothes, her jewelry. What would have happened if I'd lost it, if it had all been swept away by 137-mile-
an-hour winds? I'd still go on existing in a world of carpeting
and ceiling fans. All the objects offer is the chance to hold
what cannot be held. The comfort only comes from what's
living, what breathes.

A month later, I flew across the country to meet my friend
R in California. We ate walnut-brown bread by Monterey's
cerulean sea, ignoring the hovering haze of a massive wild-
fire. We wandered and daydreamed amid painted fences
and succulents. A woman who sat behind a drugstore
counter warned us to be careful: the winds had shifted and
the smog was choking out the oxygen. People were dying,
and I was alive and aware: of the beauty in breath, in time
spent on porches, watching bluebirds, sipping tea.

WHEN I SURRENDERED WHAT I'D WRITTEN so far to my graduate school classmates for critique, I wanted so badly a stamp of approval—some sign that it was okay, it had been long enough, I could stop trying. Instead, what I received was, "We need more of Emily."

Of course we need more of Emily. Emily was pure and unfiltered, both unafraid and nearly paranoid. Her whole world was all-or-nothing, good or bad; one of her favorite quotes was also her aspiration: "What I dream of is an art of balance." Because she was obsessed with *Calvin and Hobbes*, now Ches has a tattoo of the two characters. Our mother has a tattoo of a Matisse leaf on her wrist that matches the one Emily had. There are others who've done this—family, friends. I can't describe what it was about her. She was better than good with people but struggled to feel connected or enough. She was a mess, but friendly, talented. Anxiety slammed her against a wall when she auditioned for anything. She studied studio art and social change in college; her brain worked both creatively and critically. She couldn't not care—that curse and its blessings. She was doing her best, always, but she'd been mentally ill for ten years.

There was a fear attached to her that I carried—but I only became aware of it once she died and I had nothing left to lose. What happened, in part, involves several generations of our family. I've done my research: a postmortem investigation in which I asked questions and received answers like depression, addiction, narcissism, anxiety, OCD. Medication both self-imposed and prescribed professionally. My mother's sister's suicide when she was twenty-three.

Emily was an actress who starred in several musicals and a local low-budget horror movie. She hated her brown eyes and the space between her teeth before she got braces and, on some days, her whole body. She had a birthmark on her right arm in the shape of a neatly cracked egg. She was bouncy, wily, full of energy. The word our parents used was "animated." She looked up to me and I was mean to her, bossed her around and teased her relentlessly. Left her alone at a Halloween party so I could sleep with someone. Let my high school boyfriend have sex with me while she was in a bed across the room because I didn't know how to say no, and it was close to impossible to wake her once she was asleep (she wasn't asleep). She always forgave me—her kindness was unconditional, mostly. She helped lead a mental health support group in college—that same old story of a girl who needs support supporting others, giving to them the things she is missing, the things she doesn't know how to ask for or recognize or receive.

Emily was a magnet, a light, something incandescent, ephemeral and effervescent, like a glass filled with champagne and poetry. If each of us drank her potion we'd all hold one another too closely, bruise too easily, work assiduously without sleep. But then sometimes we wouldn't get out of bed for weeks. We'd miss therapy appointments and forget to fill our scripts and then one day, though we'd given up completely, we'd still smile and chat with our best friend while carrying a large cardboard box filled with the means to our own end through the center of a college campus. We'd create and we'd listen. We would go out of our way. We'd lose track of things, especially keys, and we'd do our best to be brave enough to share.

Should I go on forever with this listing? This is what I've been avoiding, all this missing, this knowing what it is I miss, its shape, concrete details, description. It is not a ghost or an abstraction: it is Emily, separate from me. I miss a person who does not exist. I know the hole in my body, know the things I've buried deep, the way they move and shine beneath the surface like something bioluminescent, as if I am of the sea, floating through time with nothing—no one—to tether me.

The last thirty minutes I had with my sister I spent with a toilet bowl, trying to throw up. We'd just been to the Louisiana Crawfish Festival: a meal of cheese and butter, a nauseous ride on the carnival swings. I was so completely wrapped up in my own discomfort, my own disgust, that I could hardly force myself out of the bathroom and into the car to drive her to the airport. She almost missed her flight.

I wish I had untangled myself from myself. What signs there were, I missed them. I wish I had been able to see that I was okay and she wasn't. I wanted to believe she was okay. Which is not to say I wasn't suspicious—during her last visit, I tried to guess the password to her phone while it was charging, to read her texts or emails. She was outside, smoking a cigarette. I might have seen the email if I'd succeeded, the one I found after, confirmation of a large purchase from an online gardening store. But I wouldn't have known what it meant. I might have asked Emily. Instead I asked whether she'd eaten the veggie meatballs in the freezer. She said no, but the bag was almost empty instead of nearly full. I didn't care about the food. I cared about whether she'd binged and purged, was trying to get a read. Her eyes welled up with tears when I said, "Why are you lying to me?"

It was a December day in North Carolina: cloudy and chilly and damp. A man with whom I'd been casually sleeping wanted to buy new bath towels, and I'd agreed to come with him. As we walked across a parking lot toward Bed Bath & Beyond, I said, "I used to pray for passing cars to hit me while I was out running." Maybe I was trying to share, to be honest or open. I don't know what prompted me.

He responded by telling me that once, when he was twelve, he collected pills but decided not to take them—how life has been an adventure and he would've regretted the attempt.

"Be careful how you talk about that," I warned as we walked into the store, a swirl of sad and seething.

What I heard in his words was that when someone dies by suicide a choice is made. And perhaps that is true, but my sister was sick, her mind not working properly, and as we wandered through bed toward bath, my eyes filled with tears. I blinked them back among shelves filled with folded cotton, fitted sheets, thread counts of six hundred, as if all that counts is softness, the comfort of skin against skin beneath blankets and blanket statements like "life is good." It hurts so much more to think it was chosen, to think that the belief to which I've long held fast—human agency—may have been both what she was missing (she saw no other option) and the only thing she thought she had (the ability to choose to end the pain).

It hurt the same way it had a year and a half before, on the day I climbed up Masada to watch the sun rise over Jordan and the Dead Sea. At the start of the ascent, I'd gone ahead of the group of young American Jews with whom I was traveling and jogged up the winding switchback stairs, breathing heavily in the thick summer heat of the Middle East. At the peak, the beginnings of sunbeams were breaking over waves of desert rocks and sand.

Our group's tour guide led us around the ruined fortress. He paused to retell Masada's history. I already knew that the story involves the mass suicide of Judean rebels under Roman siege—I was prepared for that fact. But as I sat on the white sand floor of a very old room, our guide began to editorialize: "In Judaism, we value life. As Jews, we choose—we make the choice—to engage in the shit of it. We choose to fight, we persist, we do not ever, ever give up. We take our chances in battle, in existence."

I wanted to leave but I stayed and built my own fort out of pebbles, tried to stay small as I wiped away tears. I searched the group's fifty faces to try to find the girl who, two nights earlier, had told me about how she'd found her father in their home after he killed himself. I wanted to meet her eyes, to know if this judgment hurt her too. A religion, stripped down to its core, disavowing them as weak, as wrong, as having had a choice.

Again came winter break, again I went up north. To my mother's house, to my father's house, to Bubbie's apartment in Philly. The sun was out. I was on a narrow strip of sidewalk, cement on a bridge. On one side, the rush of cars entering a highway, on the other, the rush of water, the Schuylkill River, several feet below the road. I was running and felt myself experience a certain curiosity, nearly an impulse to throw myself off the bridge. What would it be like to do it? I wasn't sure if it was the thought itself that filled me with fear, or the fact that I'd had the thought in the first place. It would have been so easy to alter the trajectory of my body from flat and forward to a leap, then a fall. The act itself a force of gravity.

For nearly five years I'd wondered if I did not matter to Emily, but in that moment I began to understand it differently. She knew what she'd been planning to do for weeks before she died. Some people describe a sense of peace once they've made the decision; when I saw her she did not seem especially peaceful. She seemed depressed and weakly terrified. What might she have done if she'd had a disease of the body, not the mind? That distinction, I know, is not quite right. But here's the point: Emily was not jumping out of airplanes or climbing mountains once she gave herself the knowledge that she had so little time left. She was in New Orleans, sleeping in my bed and going on walks and watching *House of Cards* with me.

The week before, she'd said, "I don't want to still be like this when I come visit."

I responded, "I know. But even if you are, I still want you here," and then she got on an airplane and came to say goodbye.

There are certain things you become more aware of when you go on living after someone close to you has died. Like the immediacy of life and the limits of existence. How being in your head is so different from being present. And you learn, too, that it is possible to exist in multiple places, on multiple planes. That it is possible to consider jumping off a bridge while you run straight ahead without change in direction or intent to live.

WHILE OUT ON A RUN one evening in February, I thought about my sister, how her birthday was approaching fast. I had to do the math—she'd be turning twenty-six. I stopped running then because I felt myself slipping away from my body. I lay down on the pavement of the path, in the dark. It felt like lying down in the snow in the middle of a street but also different—no cars, no bikes, no people, and no snow. Only trees, and it was windy; as they swayed they made a sound old and aching, as if they'd already lived once. I lay there, on the ground, the black sky so whole and wide and open above me, dark purple clouds. Placed one hand over my stomach and one over my heart and reminded myself, *You are so small, you are so small, you are so small.*

What came to me then was a memory: my cousins, sister, and me at a theme park during one of our family vacations in Maine, riding rides like the Tilt-A-Whirl and a Viking ship with the head of a dragon that swings toward the sky at improbable angles, back and forth like a pendulum. We are strapped into purple plastic seats, legs dangling, waiting to be rocketed up to the top of a tall, skinny tower and dropped down again. One cousin screams, "I'm gonna die!" over and over again.

Emily says, "If you die, I get all your clothes!"

I say, "If you die, I get your bedroom!"

The cousin says, "If you die, I get all your money!" and this is what we think of death.

We scream so loud our little barefoot bodies might explode and we hold on for dear life. When we come off the ride we are out of breath and we say, "That was so much fun! That was awesome!" and we run to whatever thrill awaits us next. Our grandparents sit on a wooden bench wearing white hats, watching without a word.

The month of March I spent trying to pretend Emily no longer affected me. Four nights before the twenty-sixth, I mixed alcohol with seltzer, showed up to a reading for school an hour late, drank another drink, then drank one more. Drove home and texted my friend H, "I don't know what I'd do without you." When I said it, I meant it—when I said it, I meant please don't leave.

And when I told H I'd been smoking cigarettes that month, she said it was okay—it was only temporary, it wasn't like I wanted to live that long anyway. I wondered if she knew how right she was. I know I am not supposed to think this way, but I grow so tired of keeping myself sane and filtered. Though I try to take care of myself, it doesn't always feel like a choice. Sometimes it feels closer to avoidance. As if I could ward off the possibility of further pain with vegetables, sufficient sleep, and exercise—as if I could manage the hole already in me and keep it from growing by any possible measure: length, width, height, depth, density.

Why are gifts given to mark anniversaries of marriage but never loss? To compare the efforts might not be so absurd; it seems to me that learning to live with a person you love and learning to live without one might both be perpetual work. At that point, it had been five years since her death, so the gift would have been wood. Which makes sense—my life had become steady, stable, sturdy. Even now, same as ever, I am fine. My sister's absence, once corrosive, is just a thing.

Until grief reappears, settles into my system and leads me to dark corners of my mind, desperate measures of my body, mornings when I pace circles around my own heart. How to force myself to connect to these feelings? How they hurt, how I feel them in my shoulders first. Sadness threads its way through my ribcage, slides down my thighs, toward the floor. I stand before a mirror and place a level on my head. Stay very still and stare. The little glass tube, neon liquid, and bubble of air reveal a slant, the extent to which I am lopsided inside. This is how I know it's real, that I'm not imagining the effects I still feel.

I am stuck here: with my limbs, my memories, my breath. What is home but a body, a sense of being seen? What is comfort but a filament between past and present with some sort of future implied? In other words, safety. In other words, care. I know it is possible to find these things without her—I know they are there. But it can be so hard to ask. So much is unknown, shaped from chaos, cannot be apprehended: thoughts, feelings, how long anything might last. So, I remind myself it will be okay, then wait for more time to pass.

And this is the process, the learning to let go. What Emily was thinking, I will never know. I imagine a longing for something different, anything different, anything that is different—any other way. I wish it could have been another way, but this is how it is, and here we are at the end, still living.

Acknowledgments

I spent nine and a half years working on this project, and many, many, many people, places, and creative works contributed to the transformation of a few journal entries into an entire book. I hope that along the way I have properly expressed how much, and in what ways, I am grateful to each person listed here—my teachers, mentors, editors, readers and listeners, friends, and family members. (Asterisks indicate those whose published work you can also read!)

Emily Bryant-Álvarez
Chase Culler*
Hope Hebenstreit
Alexis Lucido
Sarah Mackey
Jeff Oloizia*
Kara Szaflarski
Sophie Teitelbaum*
Robin Walter*

Jackson Holzberg Buckley*
Marcia Guimaraes*
Rick Anthony Furtak*
Sophie Lucido Johnson*
Paige Lester-Niles
Jeff Livesay*
Marc Morgenstern*
Patrick Nelson
Tracy Santa*
Meredith Schwengel
Ezra Siegel
The Stein family
Rachele Judd Thompson

Louise Tutelian*
Janine Utell*
Lucille Wenegieme

Jake Abrahamson*
Hannah Bridges*
Nathan Conroy*
Katelyn Freund*
Casey Gilbert*
Ashley Lee*
Cass Lintz*
Olivia Loving*
Katherine O'Hara*
Alexis Olson*
CJ Pendergast*
Aly Rodriguez*
Kaylie Saidin*
E.J. Schwartz*
Daisuke Shen*
Sophia Stid*
Rachel Taube*
Nick White*

Dan Eppstein
Scott Gloden*
Kyle Hebenstreit
Alexa Irazabal
Julie James
Julia Keller
Denali Lander
Andi Lee*
Joey McGarvey*
Mallory Pladus*
Kerri Rinaldi*
Chris Stedman*
Joseph Earl Thomas*

Kim Barnes*
Lisa Bertini
Wendy Brenner*

Mark Cox*
Melissa Crowe*
Camille Dungy*
Meg Day*
Ross Gay*
Jill Gerard*
Philip Gerard* (I wish you were here for this)
David Gessner*
Nina de Gramont*
Megan Hubbard
Rebecca Lee*
Michael Ramos*
Robert Siegel*
Emily Smith*
John Jeremiah Sullivan*
Inara Verzemnieks*

The Sundress Academy for the Arts residency at Firefly Farms, and Ge Gao.*

Daniel Slager,* Lauren Langston Klein, Briana Gwin,* Mary Austin Speaker,* and everyone else at Milkweed Editions—I feel so lucky to be part of this world.

My entire family: the Spiegels, the Schwaits, the Van Bramers, the Amalfitanos, the Liefs, the Reises. Isaac and Juno—my noodles. Thank you, over and over and over again.

And last but not least, every single person who read and responded to my writing on Medium. You let me believe this was worthwhile.

Rᴇʙᴇᴄᴄᴀ Sᴘɪᴇɢᴇʟ teaches writing in Philadelphia, where she lives with her family. She holds an MFA in creative writing from the University of North Carolina Wilmington, and *Without Her* is her first book.

milkweed
EDITIONS

Founded as a nonprofit organization in 1980, Milkweed Editions is an independent publisher. Our mission is to identify, nurture, and publish transformative literature, and build an engaged community around it.

Milkweed Editions is based in Bdé Óta Othúŋwe (Minneapolis) within Mnĭ Sota Makhóčhe, the traditional homeland of the Dakhóta people. Residing here since time immemorial, Dakhóta people still call Mnĭ Sota Makhóčhe home, with four federally recognized Dakhóta nations and many more Dakhóta people residing in what is now the state of Minnesota. Due to continued legacies of colonization, genocide, and forced removal, generations of Dakhóta people remain disenfranchised from their traditional homeland. Presently, Mnĭ Sota Makhóčhe has become a refuge and home for many Indigenous nations and peoples, including seven federally recognized Ojibwe nations. We humbly encourage our readers to reflect upon the historical legacies held in the lands they occupy.

milkweed.org

Milkweed Editions, an independent nonprofit literary publisher, gratefully acknowledges sustaining support from our board of directors, the McKnight Foundation, the National Endowment for the Arts, and many generous contributions from foundations, corporations, and thousands of individuals—our readers. This activity is made possible by the voters of Minnesota through a Minnesota State Arts Board Operating Support grant, thanks to a legislative appropriation from the arts and cultural heritage fund.

Interior design by Mike Corrao

Typeset in Baskerville

The original Baskerville was designed in 1754 by John
Baskerville in Birmingham, England. The typeface
has been praised as the intersection of classical typefaces
and the high-contrast modernists. Its digital facsimile
was re-cut in 1980 by Gunter Gerhard Lange of the
Berthold Type Foundry.